THE OLYMPIC CENTURY
THE OFFICIAL 1ST CENTURY HISTORY OF THE MODERN OLYMPIC MOVEMENT
VOLUME 8

THE
VIII OLYMPIAD

PARIS 1924
ST. MORITZ 1928

BY
ELLEN PHILLIPS

WORLD SPORT RESEARCH & PUBLICATIONS INC.
LOS ANGELES

1996 © United States Olympic Committee

Published by:
World Sport Research & Publications Inc.
1424 North Highland Avenue
Los Angeles, California 90028
(213) 461-2900

1st Century Project
The 1st Century Project is an undertaking by World
Sport Research & Publications Inc. to commemorate the
100-year history of the Modern Olympic Movement.
Charles Gary Allison, Chairman

Publishers: C. Jay Halzle, Robert G. Rossi,
James A. Williamson

Senior Consultant: Dr. Dietrich Quanz (Germany)
Special Consultants: Walter Borges (Germany), Ian
Buchanan (United Kingdon), Dr. Carl Lennartz
(Germany), Wolf Lyberg (Sweden), Dr. Norbert Müller
(Germany), Dr. Nicholas Yalouris (Greece)

Editor: Laura Foreman
Executive Editor: Christian Kinney
Editorial Board: George Constable, George G. Daniels,
Ellen Galford, Ellen Phillips, Carl A. Posey

Art Director: Christopher M. Register
Production Manager: Nicholas Pitt
Picture Editor: Debra Lemmonds Hannah
Designers: Kimberley Davison, Diane Farenick
Staff Researchers: Mark Brewin (Canada), Diana
Fakiola (Greece), Brad Haynes (Australia), Alexandra
Hesse (Germany), Pauline Ploquin (France and Senegal)
Copy Editor: Anthony K. Pordes
Proofing Editor: Harry Endrulat
Fact Verification: Carl and Liselott Diem Archives of the
German Sport University at Cologne, Germany
Statisticians: Bill Mallon, Walter Teutenberg
Memorabilia Consultants: Manfred Bergman, James D.
Greensfelder, John P. Kelly, Ingrid O'Neill
Staff Photographer: Theresa Halzle
Office Manager: Christopher Jason Waters
Office Staff: Chris C. Conlee, Brian M. Heath,
Edward J. Messler, Elsa Ramirez, Brian Rand

International Contributors: Jean Durry (France),
Dr. Antonio Lombardo (Italy), Dr. John A. MacAloon
(USA), Dr. Jujiro Narita (Japan), Dr. Roland Renson
(Belgium).

International Research and Assistance: John S. Baich
(New York), Matthieu Brocart (Paris), Alexander
Fakiolas (Athens), Bob Miyakawa (Tokyo), Rona Lester
(London), Dominic LoTempio (Columbia), George
Kostas Mazareas (Boston), Georgia McDonald
(Colorado Springs), Wendy Nolan (Princeton), Jon
Simon (Washington D.C.), Frank Strasser (Cologne),
Valéry Turco (Lausanne), Laura Walden (Rome), Jorge
Zocchi (Mexico City).

Map Compilation: Mapping Specialists Inc. Madison,
Wisconsin
Map Artwork: Dave Hader, Studio Conceptions,
Toronto
Film Production: Global Film Services, Toronto
Marketing Consultant: Robert George

Bookstore and Library Distribution:
Firefly Books Ltd.
3680 Victoria Park Avenue
Willowdale, ON M2H 3K1
(416) 499-8412
1 800-387-6192 (Canada)

U.S. Offices
230 Fifth Avenue, #1607
New York, NY 10001
1-800 803-8488 (United States)

Printed and bound in the United States by R.R.
Donnelley Co.

ISBN 0-888383-00-3 (25 volume series)
ISBN 0-888383-08-9 (Volume 8)

VIII Olympiad : Paris 1924, St. Moritz 1928.
          p.   cm. -- (The Olympic century: V.8)
    "1st Century Project is a cooperative effort between
World Sport Research & Publications Inc. and the United
States Olympic Committee to research and celebrate the 100
year history of the modern Olympic movement" -- T.p. verso.
    Includes bibliographical references and indexes.
    ISBN 1-888383-08-9
    1. Olympic Games (8th : 1924 : Paris, France) 2. Winter
Olympics (2nd : 1928 : Saint Moritz, Switzerland) I. World
Sport Research & Publications Inc. II. United States Olympic
Committee. III. Series.
GV722.1924A17.1996
796.48--dc20

CONTENTS

A MOVABLE FEAST

World War I rearranged the map of Europe, and the new political order was a favorite topic of commentators on the eve of the opening ceremony of the Games of the VIII Olympiad. Indeed, politics were unavoidable: On July 5, 1924, as the Games formally commenced, former enemies would march side by side; onetime subjects would stand next to erstwhile rulers. But at the opening of this festival of peace, amity would reign.

The ceremonies began at 10 a.m. at Notre Dame Cathedral, where the archbishop of Paris greeted participants with a sermon of encouragement. After a corresponding Protestant service, officials attended a lunch while athletes massed outside Colombes stadium.

At 3 p.m., inside the stadium, France's Republican Guard band and two choral groups rendered the host country's stirring national anthem, the "Marseillaise," and a cannon salute cued the start of the Parade of Nations. A crowd estimated at 40,000 cheered as 44 national delegations filed onto the track. The French team got the biggest ovation, of course, but the British and Americans—France's allies in the war—also drew enthusiastic applause.

The parade done, the athletes settled onto the infield (right) to hear a spate of speeches. Then French hurdler Georges André swore the Olympians' oath to uphold the rules of fair play. A flight of doves soared into the warm Parisian sky.

Classically simple, the ceremony inspired comparisons with those of ancient Greece. Not even then, one observer noted, was there a pageant "richer in glory and beauty than was the great French day in Paris."

PEERLESS PARIS, PEERLESS PAAVO

PARIS 1924

Nobody has the stillness of a great athlete in the instant before great action. Cloaked in the solitude of concentration, shot through with gathered power, calm in certain mastery, the athlete is at that moment all the beauty of the human world, the paragon of animals. No one who sees such a sight ever forgets. No one in the Olympic Stadium in Paris at 3:45 on the afternoon of July 10, 1924, ever lost the image of Paavo Nurmi as he set out to define the possible. In the midst of a humming crowd, on the fringes of a glittering, feverish city, the Finn was a still point in a turning world.

In himself, Nurmi was unprepossessing. He was short and barrel-chested, a pale-haired man with pale, cold eyes. But his coiled stillness, braced in the starting holes of a cinder track, hips up, arms rigid, a stopwatch in the palm of his right hand, held the attention. Perhaps it was the contrast between the small figure and its astounding power that

made Nurmi the legend he became. He was called a machine, but machines, in their impervious, godlike power, were still images of strength and fascination then: Artists painted them. Dancers imitated them. It was Nurmi's cold perfection that called for the epithet. When he planned his distance races—and he always planned—he was practical in his strength. This race was 1,500 meters: It was the first of the day. Then he would run 5,000 meters. But this was the time for this race.

Here was how things stood: Nurmi had set the world record for the 1,500 three weeks before, as he had for the 5,000 meters (the times were 3:52.56 for the shorter race, 14:28.2 for the longer). His competition in Paris was not formidable, by his standards. The strongest competitors were British: Henry Stallard, undefeated at home, and Douglas Lowe, who had taken the 800 meters from Stallard on July 8. Stallard was running on a seriously injured foot. Lowe was young. And in any case, the British made a point of not training seriously (a gentleman sportsman did not train seriously). There were three good Americans and another Finn who did train seriously, but not as seriously as Paavo Nurmi. The Swiss, Wilhelm Scharer, had run the fastest heat, but Nurmi, conserving energy, had taken his heats easily, running only what he needed to qualify.

Nurmi's real rival was not in this race, after all, but off resting before the 5,000 meters, to be run in just an hour's time. That rival's name was Vilho Ritola; Americans called him Willie. Earlier in the week he had taken golds in the 3,000-meter steeplechase and the 10,000-meter run—the latter a race, Nurmi bitterly believed, that should have been his. He had plans for Ritola. The 1,500 meters, the prestigious Olympic mile, was only the first step.

The gun cracked and Lowe surged ahead, leading the field at the first turn. An instant later a roar from the stands and a blue-and-white flash on his right told Lowe he was outclassed. Stopwatch in hand to keep himself on schedule, Nurmi set an outrageous pace, tempting Stallard and the Americans, Raymond Buker and Raymond Watson, to follow. Stallard and Buker, realizing that their strength for a final sprint was being sapped, quickly dropped back; the less experienced Watson hung on, losing power with every move. They finished the 500-meter circuit in 1:13.2—faster than champions would run it 40 years later on new and swifter tracks, where modern tactics would mandate slower starts and faster finishes.

In the second lap, Nurmi settled into his distinctive pace and style, his back straight, his fists relaxed and rather high. So long was his stride that his feet hardly seemed to touch the ground. The rest of the field, except for the dogged Watson, were 80 yards behind. When the bell sounded the final lap, Nurmi tossed his stopwatch onto the grass verge and, with no apparent

effort, pulled away from Watson. Glancing back with detached interest at the fight for second place, Nurmi took the last circuit in a relaxed 82 seconds: He was saving fuel, running not to set records but to win. Behind him, his face twisted with pain, Stallard managed to pull abreast of Scharer at the 10-yard mark. But Scharer moved ahead in a final burst, and Stallard collapsed across the finish line.

Nurmi had won the race in 3:53.6, an Olympic record only a second slower than his world mark. "That was not a hard race," the Finn remarked with customary hauteur. "I am not in the least tired." Then, while the unconscious Stallard was carried off by his teammates, Nurmi casually retrieved his watch, picked up his sweater, and headed for the Catacombs of Colombes—the warren of locker rooms hidden under the VIP stands. He had another race to run in less than an hour, though it hardly seemed possible that spirit and body could recover in so short a time, after such a performance.

Paavo Nurmi was in many ways the human paradigm of these Games. Born in the final years of the old era—he was 27 in 1924—he took the approach of the new: He trained in professional style, his focus obsessively fastened on winning. He was at the same time a model of the amateur, an athlete who ran for the love of it. Self-supporting, self-taught, he trained alone according to his own system, sometimes on tracks, sometimes on the dirt roads that threaded the reaches of Finland's pine forests.

It was apt that Nurmi, straddling two different epochs in sport, became a legend at the Games of the VIII Olympiad, Games that marked a transition from the old order to the new. The old was honored by the International Olympic Committee's choice of Paris to host the Games: Paris was, after all, the birthplace of Baron Pierre de Coubertin, father of the modern Olympic movement. It was Coubertin who, through sheer

WHERE THE GAMES WERE PLAYED

Colombes Stadium

Tourelles Pool

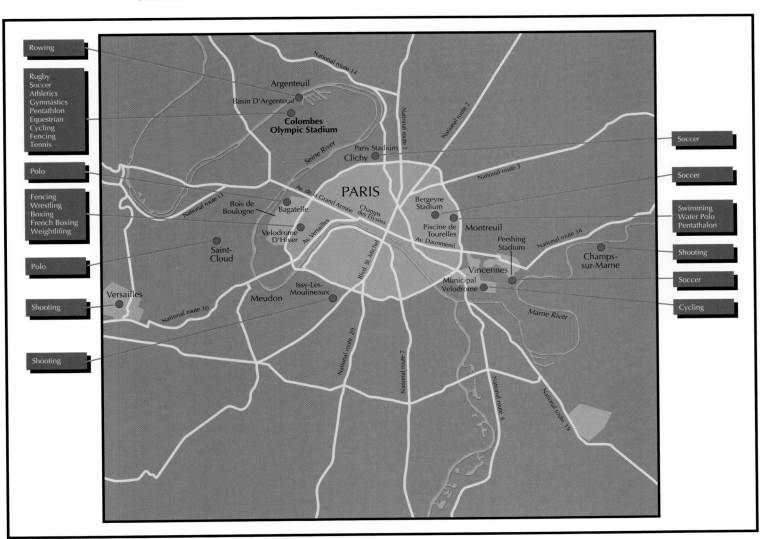

THE GAMES AT A GLANCE

	May 4-18	May 25-June 9	June 23	June 26	June 27	June 28	June 29	June 30	July 1-3	July 4	July 5	July 6-7	July 8	July 9	July 10	July 11	July 12	July 13	July 14	July 15	July 16-17	July 18	July 19	July 20	July 21	July 22	July 23	July 24	July 25	July 26	July 27
Opening Ceremony											■																				
Athletics (Track & Field)												■	■	■	■	■	■	■													
Boxing																				■	■	■	■	■							
Cycling																											■			■	■
Equestrian Sports																									■	■		■	■	■	■
Fencing					■	■	■	■				■	■	■	■	■	■	■	■												
Gymnastics																															
Modern Pentathlon																■		■	■	■											
Polo				■			■	■			■			■	■		■														
Rowing																		■	■	■	■										
Rugby	■																														
Soccer		■																													
Shooting			■	■	■	■		■	■			■	■	■																	
Swimming																		■	■	■	■	■	■	■							
Tennis																		■	■	■	■	■	■	■	■						
Water polo																		■	■	■											
Weight Lifting																											■	■	■	■	
Wrestling												■	■	■	■	■	■	■													
Yachting																			■	■	■	■				■	■	■	■	■	
Closing Ceremony																															■
Demonstration Sports																															
Canoeing																		■	■	■											
French Boxing																								■							
Children's Gymnastics																					■	■	■								
Pelote Basques																											■	■	■	■	

force of will, had breathed life back into the Games after their moribund slumber of one and a half millennia. The baron was retiring now as president of the IOC, having seen his festival transformed from a sometimes disorganized, sometimes neglected, and sometimes quarrelsome curiosity to an event with the international stature he had dreamed of—although not always in the way he had dreamed.

Paris 1924 was a monument to Coubertin's achievement, bringing together more nations and more athletes than any Games before— 3,092 competitors from 44 countries. For the first time the Games were played not according to host-country rules, but according to those standardized by the international federations governing each sport.

And the French, whose Paris 1900 Games had been chaotic at best, did themselves proud in 1924. The contests were elaborately organized and housed. The Olympic Stadium, built especially for the event, was set on a vast, weed-filled waste ground at Colombes. Colombes was an unappealing industrial suburb in Hauts-de-Seine in northwest Paris, but the facilities themselves were impressive. The main Olympic complex covered more than 40 acres. The primary stadium was flanked by a training stadium and grounds as well as by a tennis stadium and practice courts. There was an Olympic Village for the athletes—primitive, with its cramped huts, but the first of its kind. Other venues were scattered throughout Paris and around the old royal châteaux at Versailles and Fontainebleau. Bus and train schedules for the six-mile trip from the center of the city were sent to competing countries. For the opening ceremonies, the Parisians arranged a thrilling pageant of snapping flags,

IOC President Pierre de Coubertin *(second row, right)*, founder of the modern Games, and French President Gaston Doumergue *(second row, left)* leave the Sorbonne following a ceremony commemorating the 30th anniversary of the inaugural Olympic Congress. Coubertin saw his vision of an international festival of sport reach full flower during the Paris Games. It would be the last Olympics he would attend.

booming guns, circling airplanes, and soaring pigeons. The parade of athletes took almost an hour, and the teams were summoned by massed military bands playing that most stirring of anthems, the "Marseillaise."

Coubertin's beloved Paris, like the Games, was at a turning point, having survived a conflict so unimaginably terrible that it was then called the Great War. Such a cataclysm, people knew, must bring cataclysmic change. The city remained the hub of the nation, the center of transportation and finance and of intellectual life and fashion. "There was Paris," as one Parisian put it. "Outside there was a desert which was the rest of France." Chestnut and plane trees still shaded the Seine; pensioners still fished from the banks; and the tugboats, their smokestacks folded back

so that they could pass under the bridges, pulled barges up the river as before. Nursemaids still walked their charges along the gravel paths of the Luxembourg Gardens. The Comédie Française still offered the classics of the French stage, and the theaters on the boulevards still produced the light operas and farces of the past. The beautiful Mistinguett, crowned in towering feathers, still floated down her glittering staircases at the Folies Bergère, and the young boulevardier Maurice Chevalier sang his suave songs. In the early morning hours, horse-drawn carts still hauled vegetables to the great market at Les Halles from the fields of the Ile-de-France; goatherds with fresh milk to sell still brought their animals clicking over the cobblestones.

But the city was expanding at an amazing pace,

In the creative ferment of 1920s Paris, everything modern—including sport, the new rage—inspired artists. *Le Train Bleu*, a production of the Ballets Russe de Monte Carlo, was a sporting ballet set on the Riviera and named for the famed "Blue Train" that took French vacationers south. Avant-garde composer Darius Milhaud wrote the score, surrealist Jean Cocteau designed the sets, and couturier Coco Chanel, who was then busy revolutionizing women's fashion, created the costumes.

sprawling out into factory suburbs built around the nascent industries—oil, electricity, chemicals—that fueled a new machine age and brought in workers from all over France. During the war and after, Paris also attracted foreigners, not only from the French colonies in Africa and the West Indies, but also from strife-torn Russia, Armenia, and Eastern Europe. After the war, the city's sparkle (and a favorable exchange rate that permitted cheap living) drew thousands of Americans, in flight from provincialism and Prohibition.

This heady mix of elements engendered a cultural revolution—some historians compare it to the Italian Renaissance—that would define the shapes and colors of the modern age. "Paris," remarked Gertrude Stein, one of the earliest expatriates to settle there, "was where the 20th century was."

She was right. The experiments of these years—in painting, in film, in theater, in fiction—altered the way people saw the world then. They shape the way it is seen now. Pablo Picasso, Man Ray, and Joan Miró were a few of the artists who congregated in the raffish apartments of Montparnasse and laughed and drank and quarreled in its cafés—La Rotonde, Le Dôme,

La Coupole, the Closerie de Lilas. Among the writers were Colette, Jean Cocteau, Ernest Hemingway, F. Scott Fitzgerald, Ezra Pound, and James Joyce. There were jazz musicians from the United States. There were avant-garde composers like Erik Satie and Igor Stravinsky. The Ballets Russe was active then; Nijinsky was dancing. All the legends of the 20th century seemed to be in the same place at once, fashioning a brave new world.

Everything was color for their palette: war, revolutionary politics, the machine, the automobile, ships, airplanes, photography. In Paris you could find, side by side with traditional arts and entertainments, the latest American films (Colette was reviewing Westerns for *Le Figaro* in 1923), wildly experimental movies and theater, cabarets, and nightclubs. You could find, in fact, anything you wanted. The city dazzled. As the American expatriate Gerald Murphy put it: "Every day was different. There was a tension and excitement in the air that was almost physical."

A frenzied vitality pervaded everything just after the Great War. France was in the midst, for instance, of a sporting revolution that almost anybody could join, either as player or spectator.

Creative spirits of all disciplines found ideas in the work of young painters who gathered in Montmartre. Foresighted collectors and artists such as those shown here flocked to buy and sell. Some of the works that changed hands would form the nucleus of great modern art collections.

The Liffey Swim, a Dublin scene by Irish expressionist Jack Butler Yeats, won a silver medal in the Olympic art competition in Paris. Like his more famous brother, poet William Butler Yeats, the painter often incorporated scenes of Irish street life into his work, along with more exalted themes from Celtic mythology.

SPORT AND ART

The ancient Olympic Games were not only festivals of sport but also gatherings of intellectuals and artists. Pierre de Coubertin wanted the modern Games to reflect this tradition by including competitions in the arts, but the idea bore no fruit until Stockholm 1912. Even then, the contests generated little enthusiasm and drew mediocre entries. The same was true at Antwerp 1920. But the arts competition at the Paris Games initially gave the impression that the contest had matured. Artists from 23 nations submitted 189 works in five categories: painting, literature, architecture, sculpture, and music. High expectations stemmed not so much from the number of submissions, however, as from the notables who had volunteered to act as judges. Nobel Prize winners Selma Lagerlöf and

Maurice Maeterlinck agreed to read the literary works. Famed composers Igor Stravinsky and Maurice Ravel would judge the music. But the impressive jurists failed to attract correspondingly august art. Indeed, none of the musical entries was deemed worthy of a medal, and in architecture the highest award given was the silver. That went to Hungarian Alfréd Hajós for his design for a sport stadium. A Greek, Konstantinos Dimitriades, won the gold medal for sculpture. His creation, *Finnish Discus Thrower*, now rests in the Olympic Museum in Lausanne, Switzerland. Luxembourg's Jan Jacoby, who created a triptych entitled *Study of Sport*, won a gold for painting. And Frenchman Charles Guyot claimed top honors for literature with *Summer Olympics*, a series of poems.

The rich had tennis clubs, yacht clubs, and race-tracks. For the working class, who'd had a certain amount of leisure since the eight-hour day became law in 1919—there was soccer and rugby. Boxing inspired fervent attention. According to Simone de Beauvoir, when the American Jack Dempsey knocked out the French champion Georges Carpentier in their 1919 fight, people wept in the Paris streets. Cycling had long been a national passion. In those years, before automobile traffic made it impossible, there were races throughout the country; and the Tour de France, established in 1903, was the sporting event of the year, then as now. Even those with little money for equipment could do something athletic: On summer nights in the Paris suburbs, you could always find a foot race.

And in the Olympic Stadium at Colombes, in the new swimming pool at the Porte de Lilas, in the old Vélodrome d'Hiver in the 15th Arrondissement, and at its other venues, Paris 1924 reflected the spirit of the age, as all Olympic Games do. New political thought—thought that would dominate most of the century—occupied the International Olympic Committee: The growing power and pugnacity of the working class—the French Communist Party was formed in 1924—manifested itself as proposals for workers' games; the emancipation of women, speeded by the war, was reflected in plans for separate women's games. (Women already competed in some Olympic contests, but only semiofficially. Coubertin and his colleagues, men of an earlier era, didn't much care for the idea.) Greater awareness of northern sports resulted in the establishment of Olympic Winter Games.

And, as in every Olympiad of the century, the tricky issues of amateurism and nationalism permeated the Games.

Coubertin's vision of Olympism was decidedly democratic, a dream of bringing together the best young athletes of the world, regardless of race, class, or economic status. These youths would compete solely for the love of sport, without thought of recompense. In that sense, they would be amateurs.

But Coubertin's dream was born in an age when European sport was dominated by the ideals of 19th-century Britain, ideals that defined amateurism somewhat differently. Central to the British definition was the image of the gentleman sportsman, for whom athletics were but a part of a well-balanced character and a well-balanced life. It went without saying that a gentleman sportsman never played for money. But it was also essential that he did not put unseemly emphasis on perfecting his skills. Thus in 1924 the definition of amateurism centered as much on training style—professional training remained in question—as on the issue of money. The British, who rightly believed that they had invented modern sport, sent to Paris their gentleman amateurs, drawn mostly from their great universities. (Although one of their stars had a professional coach, the instructor wasn't permitted in the stadium.) The Americans, on the other hand, were well ahead on training: Their team, 450 people strong, arrived with a huge complement of managers and coaches—a dozen for track and field alone.

As for nationalism: Even though the IOC discouraged it, everyone kept national scores. It was worse than that: The nations couldn't even agree on how to score. The French used a different scoring system from everyone else. Fervent nationalism, which had done so much to bring about the Great War, now helped inspire a series of incidents—in rugby, in boxing, in fencing, and in walking—that ranged from the shameful to the ludicrous. Sports reporters in every country had a field day criticizing other nations' standards.

Fractious though it was, this sporting ferment nourished a series of legendary performances. Paris 1924 glittered with 20th-century icons—people famous in sport, and people whose sporting prowess preceded renown in other fields. Young John Weissmuller, a poor boy from

Finland's Vilho Ritola makes a tepid bid to shake hands with his nemesis, Nurmi. Though countrymen, the two track stars were not friendly.

American mothers how to care for their infants, then emerged in his old age as a radical political activist. John B. Kelly, a Philadelphia businessman and political power, won the double sculls, but he is more famous for fathering Grace Kelly.

American swimmer Gertrude Ederle was a lesser light in the Games, but a short time after them she became the first woman to swim the English Channel. American tennis player Helen Wills was just beginning her career as queen of Wimbledon. In track and field, the American Clarence de Mar of Boston became the marathon runners' symbol in his own country, even though no Olympic victory ever graced his career. And De-Hart Hubbard, one of eight blacks in his huge class at the University of Michigan, was the first American of his race to win an individual Olympic gold. Britons Harold Abrahams and Eric Liddell dominated the sprinting events. Their feats are preserved—beautifully if inaccurately—in the 1981 film *Chariots of Fire*.

Of them all, Paavo Nurmi was perhaps the most driven. Devoted only to running, he rarely smiled and rarely talked, and when he did talk he was unendearing. Asked by a breathless reporter how it felt to be an Olympic champion whose exploits had brought glory to Finland, he barked, "I run for myself, not Finland."

Running for himself—his heart beating 40 times a minute, his clean stride eating the miles—Nurmi was a Finnish hero by the end of 1923. As a tyro at the 1920 Antwerp Games, he had won three gold medals and a silver, the last in a 5,000-meter contest won by Joseph Guillemot of France. After that, Nurmi made himself a new training schedule. He didn't care for second place. By the end of 1923 the work had paid off: He had set six world records for distances between 1,000 and 10,000 meters. It was clear that he could win any prize he wanted in 1924. Always a planner, he decided on five: the 1,500, 5,000,

Chicago, won three individual gold medals in the swimming pool. He went on to an athletic career that included an astounding 67 world records, but he usually is remembered for his chest-thumping yell as Tarzan in the movies. Benjamin Spock, rowing for Yale and America in the prestigious eight-oar shells, became the pediatrician who taught at least two generations of

and 10,000 meters; the punishing 10,000-meter cross-country; and the cross-country team race.

Then things began to go wrong. The Paris Olympic Organizing Committee, in an attempt to stop the Finns from dominating Paris 1924 (as the Finns had dominated Antwerp 1920), scheduled the 1,500- and 5,000-meter race starts half an hour apart. Furious, the Finns protested, and the interval was changed to a still-stingy 55 minutes—a margin yet narrow enough, it would seem, to thwart Nurmi and Company. Next, on Easter Sunday, 1924, Nurmi fell during a run on an icy road, lacerating his knee and damaging the kneecap. He couldn't even walk for three weeks. But before the knee was fully healed he began to train again, first limping along the track, then running, but at drastically reduced times.

At this point, Vilho Ritola came home. The 28-year-old Ritola had, like thousands of his compatriots, moved to the United States early in the century. He was in his teens then; in his early twenties he began running, carving out an impressive career in his adopted country. Living—and training—in America was a good deal easier

than in Finland, but Ritola had wanted to represent his homeland in the Olympic Games. So he returned, to become a thorn in the side of Paavo Nurmi. In the May Olympic trials, Ritola broke Nurmi's 10,000-meter world record. Then he won the 5,000 meters. Nurmi, with his injured leg, qualified in the 1,500 and 3,000 meters, but the times, for him, were slow.

Nurmi's response was to push his training to sterner levels, and in a few weeks he showed the world the results: In a Helsinki meet that was a rehearsal for the upcoming Paris Games, he ran his world-record 1,500 meters, rested 55 minutes, then ran a world-record 5,000. Stung by a press report that, even in top form, he could never beat Ritola in the 10,000 meters, Nurmi also ran a private and unofficial trial heat at that distance, clocking in at 29:58.0. It was a time he would never again equal, nor could any other runner of his day touch it. Nevertheless, Finnish officials decided against letting him make the race in Paris. Nurmi would sit out the 10,000 meters, which would begin the distance racing at the Games. That was for Ritola; the Finns didn't

Ritola leaps a water barrier in the 3000-meter steeplechase, a contest that takes its name from early British cross-country races whose routes were marked by church steeples. Ritola won this race, as he did the 10,000 meters, and with Paavo Nurmi, the 3,000-meter team race. His only losses came in the head-to-head competition with Nurmi.

Paavo Nurmi checks his stopwatch in the early stages of the 5,000-meter race. Teammate Vilho Ritola is just a few paces behind—reflecting the usual order of finish for these two rivals.

want both their stars exhausted at the start.

In Paris, having won the 1,500 meters, Nurmi had a massage and (legend claims) a nap. At 4:45 he was crouched in his starting holes once more, flanked by a rested Ritola, who hadn't run that day, and by Edvin Wide, a fine Swedish runner who had challenged Nurmi before, although not in an Olympic race and not successfully. Nurmi wasn't particularly worried about Wide: Wide wasn't the man to beat at 5,000 meters.

A 19-year-old French runner, Lucien Dolques, led off at the pistol, but at the start of the second 500-meter lap Ritola and Wide broke out, setting a horrific tempo designed to exhaust Nurmi. Dolques followed. Unperturbed, stopwatch in hand, Nurmi let them draw 40 yards ahead. Dolques faded at the beginning of the third lap, and Nurmi began to move up; by 2,000 meters, Wide, Nurmi, and Ritola were 60 yards ahead of the Frenchman. Wide faded and fell back at 2,500 meters.

Now Nurmi and Ritola ran alone against each other, Ritola one yard behind, their battle watched by a screaming crowd and by every athlete and official of every competition who could make it to trackside. The contrast in style alone was worth it. Nurmi, expressionless and erect, maintained a glacial calm and his graceful, long, rolling stride. He never looked back. He hardly needed to. With Ritola breathing down his neck, he knew exactly where the man was. Ritola ran bent over, and his gait was a kind of leap; his hands swung low and rather clumsily. Always a sufferer when he ran, he suffered here: His face was a rictus of clenched teeth and bulging veins.

At the start of the last 500-meter circuit, Nurmi glanced at his watch and dropped it to one side, his unnerving signal that his race was won. When Ritola quickened his pace in a final, desperate bid to pass, Nurmi increased his own speed. He never allowed the maddening yard's gap to close. He finished in 14:31.2, an Olympic record, with Ritola two seconds behind. A reporter saw them leave the track: Ritola clapped Nurmi on the back and grinned; Nurmi turned his head—that was all. They walked together to the Catacombs of Colombes, but as one observer put it, everyone—runners and spectators—saw the tension between them. It had pushed Nurmi to his astonishing double victory, a feat no one had done before, and no one has done since. He was Peerless Paavo, the Phantom Finn.

What made Paavo run? What made him the distance runner that he was? The answer lay in himself and in his culture, and also in a fine irony of the modern Olympics. The Games were founded in a period of clear class distinctions, the time of the gentleman amateur. Yet they have, from the first marathon at Athens 1896, been a source of democratic opportunity to those for whom sport must be everything. In tests of skill and endurance, even the most obscure can win lasting fame.

That was true of Nurmi, as of many others. He grew up in a hard country, in hard times. Finland, high in the remote north between Sweden and Russia, was wild country until about 1200, a vast, icy wilderness traversed by hunting tribes whose people were a mixture of immigrant Europeans and nomadic tribes from east of the Ural Mountains. They spoke, and speak, a language only remotely related to any other. (It is often said to be distantly related to Hungarian, but the relationship is about as close as that between English and Farsi.)

By 1200 Finland had become a province of Sweden and would remain so for 600 years until, during one of the interminable wars of the period, it was annexed by Russia as a grand duchy. By the mid-19th century the Finns were defining themselves, retrieving their own mythology, and agitating for independence. They gained it only with the collapse of the Russian armies during the revolution of 1917 and the First World War. As in many emerging nations, a bloody civil war followed. The rest of Europe was tearing itself to shreds, but in the north, Finn was fighting Finn, communist fighting democrat, the one supported by Russia and the other by Sweden and Germany, all of whom had interests in the region. The war—Nurmi fought in it as a young conscript—was finally resolved in 1920 by a treaty that established parliamentary democracy. War brought famine in the countryside, widespread malnutrition, disease, and poverty, alleviated only by the strong cultural identity—and determination—of the Finns themselves.

All of this formed the background of Nurmi's childhood and youth, which were hard indeed. His father, a carpenter, died when the boy was 12. The family slid into destitution, its six members living in a single room. Nurmi went to work as an errand boy, pushing delivery carts up the hills of Turku, the old coastal capital in the southwest.

Athletics were his way out. Finland loved athletes. Central to Finnish identity is the hardy countryman's harmony with his magnificent landscape—islands, sea, pine forests, lakes, tundra. In a nation with few rails and fewer roads, where transportation was most often by foot and ski, hardiness was crucial, and athleticism was part of that hardiness. It was—and is—an expression of *sisu*, an untranslatable word describing the Finn's independence, solitary character, and toughness in the face of adversity.

Finnish runners—exemplars of sisu—dominated the Olympic Games from as early as Stockholm 1912, when the country was still a Russian grand duchy. (Finns on that team won 23 medals, compared with the Russian contingent's three; pointedly, the Finns left a 150-foot gap between themselves and their Russian teammates at the opening ceremonies' parade, and displayed the Finnish flag at the awards.) The star of those Games was Hannes Kolehmainen, the original Flying Finn, the first of the great Finnish distance runners. His victory showed the young Paavo

A portrait of the Nurmi family in 1924 shows an unsmiling Paavo *(right rear)* with his mother, brother, and two sisters. Absent is Johan Nurmi, Paavo's father, who died in 1910. Nurmi took his father's death hard, though it may have helped spur him to greatness. A friend said of Nurmi that running was "a replacement for his father."

Nurmi what was possible. Nurmi began to train.

In the early part of the century, knowledge about distance training was rudimentary. At 17, Nurmi joined an athletic club—necessary for entering competitions—where observation of other runners and his own obsessive nature led him to plan his program of development. He would follow it and patiently modify it over the next years, running in the mornings before work and in the evenings afterward. Ever solitary, he was secretive about his training system. When queried, he gave contradictory accounts; when anyone tried to join him—even someone from his own club—Nurmi simply outpaced him. He wasn't prepared to help other people; Paavo Nurmi trained alone.

In the years of Nurmi's greatness, many commentators speculated on its sources, most homing in on his alleged diet of raw, smoked fish and black bread. (In fact, Nurmi seldom if ever ate either one; his staple was oatmeal.) Most probably, however, his private regimen was a precursor of interval training; that is, short, hard sprints interspersed with distance runs and recovery periods.

The result of such training is maximum aerobic power: a respiratory and circulatory system—strong lungs, big heart and blood vessels—that delivers oxygen to the muscles as efficiently and as long as possible, so that the runner need put minimum reliance on reserves.

Interval training is what one version of his 1924 workouts seems to resemble: "After his morning walk of 10 to 12 kilometers and some gym work, he rested for an hour before going to the track," according to a contemporary account. "There he ran four or five furious sprints of 80 to 120 meters, then a fast 400 to 1,000 for time, followed by 3,000 to 4,000 meters with the last lap always very fast. In the evening he ran 4,000 to 7,000 meters across country, punishing himself at the finish. He closed with four or five sprints." It should be noted that this was in May, in Finland: The light lingers until after 11 p.m. then, but the temperatures still are very cold, and the roads often icy.

The stopwatch, which he began using after Antwerp 1920, told him his speed. A distance runner, unlike a sprinter, must run at a constant

Nurmi demonstrates one of the 16 exercises that made up his daily training regimen. The entire routine, which took only 10 minutes, was central to his training.

pace—rationing his power—and this was done best, he found, by timing himself over fractions of the course. Nurmi, who mapped out every step of every race, needed the stopwatch to tell him whether he was on target. The effect on other runners, especially when the watch was discarded, may be imagined.

Training this way was doubtless the source of Nurmi's great calm. Running seemed to produce in him an unearthly detachment, a state that University of Chicago psychologist Mihaly Csikszentmihaly would later term "flow." Flow is the condition of joyful awareness of a perfect match between capability and the demands of the situation. Knowing he is operating exactly at his limit—never under or beyond it—gives an athlete enormous freedom and concentration; it releases him from fear and the petty demands of self. It gives him the matchless pleasure of mastery.

Never was Nurmi's mastery more perfectly displayed than at Paris 1924 in the 10,000-meter cross-country race. Held on Saturday, July 12, this contest was a nightmare of endurance. The temperature that day was officially recorded as 86 degrees Fahrenheit—but the meteorologists' instruments hung in the countryside, at the new Le Bourget Airport, and they hung in the shade. At Colombes, the temperature ranged as high as 113 degrees, and there was almost no shade. Heat squatted on the cruel course, on the stony, thistle-covered paths that ran interminably out along the Seine past a fume-belching energy plant, and back through dusty, baking streets of small stucco houses, of factories, dingy cafés, and *bar-tabacs.*

Forty-two runners started the brutal distance race just outside the stadium. Inside, relay heats continued. Half an hour after the cross-country pistol, however, when word came that the competitors were approaching, the heats were suspended. The crowd fell silent.

The shouting began when Paavo Nurmi ran through the Marathon Gate and jogged partway around the track to the finish. He was sweating,

but otherwise composed and running in his usual straight-backed, rhythmic style, his face impassive as always. His time was 32:04.8. There was a pause. Then Ritola arrived, also alone. He crossed the line, looking like death. Observing him, Nurmi gave a thin smile.

No one was prepared for what happened next, and pandemonium broke loose in the stands. An American, Earl Johnson, reeled in, followed by a Briton, who staggered across the line and collapsed, unconscious. Behind these two came a grotesque trickle of heatstroke-maddened zanies. One, a Spaniard, came in clutching the air, running headfirst into a concrete wall. He fell, covered in blood. Another competitor entered and turned the wrong way. Corrected, he stopped, swaying. The crowd roared support, and officials ran up to catch him. Pushing them off, he fell to his hands and knees and began to twist in small circles on the ground, propelled by feet that scrabbled in the dust. Two other runners lurched blindly into each other and fell in a tangled heap. Several contestants ran backwards.

Spectators groaned. Stretcher-bearers rushed to the fallen, then fanned out through the countryside to search for other casualties. There were plenty of them, runners who had fallen in the dirt, gasping and vomiting. Most were hospitalized. Meanwhile, sportswriters counted. The London *Times* summed it up: "Of 42 men who started, only 18 entered the stadium; only 12 crossed the line." The rest had fallen along the route. Among the casualties was the Swede, Edvin Wide, who had led with Ritola and Nurmi until he collapsed. Critically ill, he was rushed to a hospital. It was rumored that he had died, although, fortunately, this was not the case.

All in all, the carnage was heartbreaking. It put an end to Olympic cross-country racing forever.

It did not, however, faze Paavo Nurmi. He went on the next day to win, with Ritola and Elias Katz, the 3,000-meter team race. It was his fourth gold medal: He had won one more than

Nurmi crests a stone fence in the 10,000-meter cross-country. The barriers and the killing heat left him unaffected, but they claimed so many other casualties that the race would never be run again in the Olympic Games.

Ritola. When he returned to Finland, just to make a point in his stubborn way, Nurmi ran 10,000 meters in 30:06.2 minutes—a world record, and, more important, a world mark 17 seconds faster than Ritola's.

In his long career, Nurmi would win nine gold and three silver Olympic medals. He would tour America in 1925, running 52 races and winning 51 (the only loss was an 800-meter race, shorter than his customary distances). He would lose to Ritola at Amsterdam 1928. But his greatest loss would come in 1932, when the International Amateur Athletic Federation, the governing body of track, would disqualify him from the Los Angeles Games on the ground of professionalism. The IAAF would allege that he charged excessive expenses in traveling to various competi-

tions. Nurmi took it hard. There were reports—difficult to credit—that the frosty Finn actually wept at the news of his ouster. "My heart bleeds to end a career by winning the marathon," he said. Surely an Olympic marathon victory would have been within his grasp, but now this final laurel would elude him.

The IAAF's somewhat vague accusations incensed the Finns, who did not disqualify him: Paavo Nurmi was a national hero, and his country honored him for it. In the ancient city of Turku, where the river Aura rolls toward its coastal castle and the island-studded Baltic Sea, Finland erected a statue of her matchless runner. Living in Turku, Nurmi would see himself in bronze for almost 50 years.

Whether his triumphs gave him joy is hard to

tell: Nurmi's comments tended to be bleak. He married and fathered a son, but the marriage ended in divorce after only a year. Financially, he did well as he aged. He was a paper hanger by trade, and Finland's wealthy vied for the cachet of having the famed Nurmi work in their homes. Later he lived comfortably from property investments in Turku and profits from a sporting goods store. He continued running competitively into his late thirties, and he coached some of the fine young Finnish runners who would try to follow in his giant strides. But gout, rheumatism, and time inexorably eroded a body that once—so finely tuned and so responsive—had made the whole world marvel. Gradually, Nurmi faded from international view.

But his country never forgot him. When the Games came to Helsinki in 1952, thousands of Finns watched in the stadium as the Olympic torch made the final leg of its journey from Greece. The name of the runner who would bear that torch on its last lap in Helsinki was secret, but a murmur started among viewers close to the track as he ran, small and straight and graceful. The murmur became an endless, deafening roar as the runner approached the Olympic cauldron, and a single word flashed on the scoreboard:

"Nurmi"

Peerless Paavo's feats in Paris tend to obscure those of his compatriots now, but the Finnish accomplishments then were enough to stimulate a babble of international speculation. In Paris, for instance, Vilho Ritola had won three golds (counting the team race) and two silvers. He would have earned mythic stature himself, except that he was fated to run in the shadow of the Phantom.

At Paris 1924 the Finns also conquered in the marathon and in less spectacular events such as the javelin, the pentathlon, and wrestling. They naturally attracted attention, especially in the United States, jealous of its championship status. As the *New York Times* put it, comparing the 12 U.S. and 10 Finnish golds, "The Finns are the all round if not the actual champions of the Games." America, it pointed out, had 105 million people from whom to cull its finest athletes, Finland only three million.

There ensued lengthy newspaper discussions about the little country and the prowess of its people. Finns living in America, especially reporters on the Finnish-language newspapers of the large colony in Duluth, Minnesota, found themselves in particular demand for comments.

Reporters offered facts and opinions ranging from the ethnological—remarks about the Finns' "inheritance from the Asian steppes"—to the even more wildly fanciful. There was the business about the spartan national diet of black bread and raw fish, of course, and American readers were also introduced (in various curious and colorful accounts) to the Finnish sauna, theretofore virtually unheard of. Most all Finns, some stories went, baked themselves medium rare in huts filled with hot rocks, then flogged themselves with birch switches until they were the color of lobsters. It was also widespread Finnish custom, it was said, to take ice baths each morning, followed by vigorous rolls in the snow. In such arcane practices, the papers said, lay the secret of the Finns' superhuman endurance.

Tiring of patronizing and ill-informed sportswriters, Leonard Cline of the *New York World* reminded his audience that Finns had triumphed in many fields: There were architects such as Eliel Saarinen and composers such as Jean Sibelius, not to mention pianists and singers. Leaving no attitude untouched, Cline added that "not only Finland's hard-muscled athletes but every single person in that country—little children, frail mothers and maids, even feeble old men and tremulous women quavering through the last pale years of life—goes through, day after day, the ordeal of talking in Finnish. After

Judge's badge for the 1924 Games.

that, why should one be surprised at anything the Finns accomplish?"

It was left to the Finns themselves to point out that although Paavo Nurmi was a miracle, even to them, their climate and their history demanded stamina from all their citizens. Ever seeking to inculcate that virtue, Finland had had universal, compulsory physical education for a quarter of a century by the time Nurmi arrived at Paris 1924. As for the diets and training regimens of Finnish athletes, those were derived from American menus and methods.

Nevertheless, comparisons and speculation continued as long as the Games were fresh in everyone's minds. Despite IOC discouragement, commentary revolved around national point scores and standings. These varied. For instance, in an article published in September of 1924, the American journal *Current Opinion* ranked the leading victors of the Games as the U.S., France, Sweden, Great Britain, and Finland. When revised to take population size into account, the order changed to Norway, Finland, Sweden, Switzerland, and Uruguay. Great Britain came in 12th in this version, the U.S. 14th. This just proved, the writer added, that "Scandinavians and Swiss are the people of the most athletic physique."

The IOC could no more prevent nationalistic scorekeeping then, after one world war, than it can now, after two. The more prestige the Games acquired and the greater the Olympic mystique, the more prestige for winning countries. Not uncommonly over the years, national pride has deteriorated to ugly chauvinism during the Games, and international incidents have occasionally occurred. So it was at Paris 1924. As

NEW WORLD, NEW SOCCER

The Olympic soccer tournament in Paris was the first true worldwide showcase for the sport, and it would develop into a contest between Old World and New. The New World interloper in the 22-team field was Uruguay, the first squad from South America to enter Olympic competition. The quality of South American soccer was an unknown, so Uruguay's first game, against a solid team from Yugoslavia, caused little interest. However, the 5,000 fans who did bother to watch the match were treated to a 7-0 blowout by the South Americans, and the Uruguayan team instantly became the talk of the tournament. Foremost among its players was José Andrade, dubbed "the Black Pearl" by the press. Andrade *(right)* was the first black player to grace an Olympic soccer pitch. A right midfielder, he controlled the tempo of games like a choreographer, reflecting, perhaps, his work

as a dancer and musician back in Montevideo. Andrade was a masterful ball handler who could rush through entire defensive units and pinpoint open teammates with his passes. He led Uruguay's march to the semifinals, where the newcomers held on to beat a tough squad from the Netherlands 2-1. In the other semifinal match, Switzerland was having pregame problems—although not with rival Sweden. Because of poor planning, the Swiss found themselves stranded in Paris with no money. A public appeal back in Switzerland raised the needed cash, and it turned out to be a good investment: Switzerland edged Sweden 2-1. The finals were a clash between the artistic and individual style of the South Americans and the focused attack that characterized the European style. New World overcame Old as the creativity of the Uruguayan players won the day, downing the Swiss 3-0.

always, the tensions that year were fueled by time and place and politics. The coruscating energy that shaped Parisian life in the 1920s was a reaction, at least in part, to the nightmare of World War I and its aftermath.

It is difficult now, surveying the green and gold riches of the French countryside, to imagine what it was then. When the guns fell silent in 1918, northeastern France lay in smoke-blackened ruins, a wasteland of rubble, blasted tree trunks, and mud where nothing would grow. Perhaps worst was Verdun, the country's historical eastern bastion. Verdun would become the national symbol of suffering. Intending to demoralize the French—"bleed them white" was the generals' phrase—the Germans attacked Verdun in 1916. In the year-long battle of attrition that followed, at least 400,000 Frenchmen —and perhaps as many as half a million—died. Parts of bodies were still surfacing 50 years later.

Verdun was only one battle. In all the battles of the Great War, France lost a generation: Some 1.4 million people, more than a quarter of her young men, were killed; another million were

permanently crippled. And afterward, reminders were everywhere. Every family wore black mourning. Every village had a stone monument naming its sons, *mort pour la France*. Those sad lists of names often included whole families of brothers and cousins. Every form of public transport had seats reserved for *mutilés de guerre*.

At war's end, a shattered France wanted revenge and she wanted national security: She wanted Germany punished and hobbled. She wanted allies. She wanted money. The French had financed the war not by taxation, but by expensive loans—$7 billion just from the U.S.— and they demanded that, as reparation, the Germans pay all the debts as well as the costs of restoring France's devastated factories and cities and scarred farmland.

But the Treaty of Versailles, which ended the war, left the French feeling swindled. The treaty did indeed levy heavy loads of debt and guilt on defeated Germany, but it had no teeth. The U.S. Congress, weary of Europe's bloody politics, refused to ratify it, and the British wouldn't support it either. From a practical point of view, the

question of reparations remained unresolved.

France began rebuilding with the help of more loans as it gradually became clear that, barring renewed hostilities, no war debts would be paid by prostrate and inflation-ridden Germany. Inevitably, international markets soon lost faith in the indebted, overvalued French franc. Money flowed out of the country. In 1923, unsupported, France invaded Germany's Ruhr Valley to force a settlement of the reparations issue. Germany dissembled and passively resisted. The invasion, such as it was, ended in a sullen standoff in the Ruhr and rampant inflation in France.

Obviously, the nation would have to retrench. Costs were soaring, but taxes would have to be raised—by as much as 20 percent. Feeling betrayed by their allies and contemptuous of their disheveled government, the people prepared to change their ineffective leadership in the 1924 elections.

Not that the battered citizens had lost their distinctive pride in France and in all things French, however. France had, after all, emerged from the Great War as the only Continental power: Every other was in a shambles. As fair as ever, France endured, the undimmed cultural beacon and chief ornament of the West—and not only in French eyes, as the flood of visitors and the champagne sparkle of Parisian creative life showed.

It was therefore time for celebration, and the 1924 Games provided the perfect opportunity. The Olympics would be the most stylish of international displays, a festival of youth and renewed vigor after the bleak years of death and destruction. Successful Games demanded more than good facilities and able athletes, however. Another requirement was large and enthusiastic ticket-buying crowds, and that meant snaring a big working-class audience.

Rugby was the answer. This rugged version of football, beloved of blue-collar Frenchmen, had been a major crowd pleaser for 40 years. France had a fine rugby team. Envisioning a French victory hailed by throngs of cheering French citizens, Paris' Olympic Organizing Committee planned a rugby competition to be played five weeks before the official opening of the Games. Pre-Games rugby matches were not unusual in Olympic planning, and in Paris the tournament would surely whet interest in the coming main event. It was bound to be a success—as long as worthy rivals for the French team could be found.

Therein lay a problem. Great Britain, the home of rugby, declined to play, finding the May date inconvenient. In fact, the only European team that signaled its intention to compete was Romania's. So the organizing committee invited the California Rugby Union to field a team.

In America, rugby had had a checkered history. The descendant of primitive forms of soccer and the ancestor of American football, the game evolved around 1840 at the British public school of the same name. It was introduced to the San Francisco Bay Area in 1904 as a means of deflecting college athletes from the savageries of American football, which, in those days, was a carnage-strewn free-for-all. Football was, in fact, banned in California for a time, giving rugby a firm toe-hold there. The state fielded a team at Antwerp 1920 that won the gold medal. Then interest seemed to fade.

But the Californians' response to the 1923 invitation was quite enthusiastic. The American Olympic Committee (the AOC, a precursor of the USOC) gave the team its blessing, but no cash. Nevertheless, money was raised swiftly through public donations. Rugby Union manager Sam Goodman and coach Charles Austin

rounded up what players they could from the championship Antwerp team and sent out a general call for football players around the country to try out. Volunteers flocked in, and by spring Goodman and Austin had a team in very good shape, but with some of its members short of practice in real competition. In search of experience, the California contingent set out in April for England. The British were delighted to help out. They noted that the Americans were "big, rugged, hugely aggressive, long on strength and endurance but short on finesse." Well aware that the French were long on finesse, the English made sure the newcomers learned—in games with their own best teams—how to counter it. They also treated their American cousins in

American and French players clash at Colombes stadium in a pre-Olympic contest. They are playing the exclusively amateur version of the game known as rugby union. Difficult as those who saw the match would find it to believe, the professional game—known as rugby league and introduced in 1895—was designed to be faster and rougher and thus more exciting for spectators.

princely fashion. Everyone was pleased.

Unfortunately, this happy state of affairs began deteriorating the moment the Americans crossed the English Channel. There were visa problems and maddening bureaucratic delays at Calais, where the team had to cool its heels for six rainy hours. Finally allowed into France, some of the Americans soon concluded that they would have been better off kept out. "Without going into details about our stay in the French capital, it is only necessary to remark that we were accorded anything but hospitable treatment," a sour Sam Goodman mused later. "In fact, many times we were treated with open hostility." Even so, the Americans soldiered on, training twice a day and behaving themselves. As player Charlie Dow put

it, "We never did anything wrong: no excessive drinking, clean living, and no women." By the time the matches started, they were ready.

As the Paris Olympic Organizing Committee had hoped, there was an enormous turnout of some 40,000 rugby fans for the round of contests. The French and Americans took turns beating the only other team involved—the hapless Romanians—but the real interest clearly lay in the Franco-American match, which was held on May 17, a hot day with random showers that turned the field to mud.

Small, agile, and subtle, the French were local 20-to-1 favorites ("for about five minutes," Goodman would remark). It was soon clear that the French players, while valiant, were hopelessly

GYMNASTICS

Gymnastics were among the earliest forms of organized exercise. Even so, a universal system of drills had not yet evolved by the time of the Paris Games. Most of the apparatus used in 1924 were familiar: horizontal bar, rings, side horse vault, parallel bars, and the pommel horse, but the floor exercises had not yet appeared. Instead, athletes performed a rope climb and a jump known as the long horse vault. Competition was for men only. Some of the early gymnastics organizations had developed their exercises as a complement to military training. As a consequence, gymnastics were very tribal, and the national pride implicit in the sport was on display at Paris. The Sokol club of Yugoslavia (*above*), composed entirely of Slovenes, marched into the tournament wearing traditional ethnic costumes. So did several other teams, but Yugoslavia had a special reason for the display: World War I had brought it independence from the Austrian Empire, and Paris 1924 was the first time it would compete as a nation. The Games would also produce Yugoslavia's first Olympic champion, gymnast Leon Stukelj (*second from right*), winner on the horizontal bar and in the all-around competition. Stukelj would go on to win a gold medal and a bronze at Amsterdam 1928, and he would end his long and distinguished Olympic career at Berlin 1936. There, at the age of 36, he would win his final medal, a silver in the rings. Stukelj would live to see his homeland of Slovenia secede from a disintegrating Yugoslavia in 1991 and compete as an independent nation at Barcelona 1992.

Finland's Jonni Myrrä launches the javelin in defense of his title from Antwerp 1920. Myrrä would repeat as champion in Paris, though his best effort would have placed him only fourth four years earlier.

outclassed. The Americans outweighed them by 30 pounds a man, and—unlike the French—the U.S. players were in peak condition from months of intensive training. Moreover, the Americans had been schooled by the British to counter French speed with a close, thrusting, highly aggressive game. By the end of the first half, the score was only 3-0, but the French had lost two men to injuries, and the rest of their players were limp with exhaustion.

Desperate in the second half, the French began to foul. Again and again, the Americans scored. Cheers from the stands greeted every foul; boos and hisses greeted every score. As play progressed, noise increased. At game's end, a French player taking advantage of a fumble fell on the ball behind the American goal to produce the only French points. The Americans had humiliated their hosts 17-3.

Then the fights began—not on the field, where the players were amicably shaking hands—but in the stands. Eight foolhardy American art students, who had been screaming all along and who should have had more sense, jeered the low French score. Enraged Frenchmen responded by beating them bloody with canes. Two of the Americans had to be hospitalized.

At this worst of all possible moments, a band struck up "The Star Spangled Banner." The crowd, its nasty mood nearing critical mass, booed the U.S. anthem for 10 minutes. Taking no chances, police escorted the American players out a side door. "Who needs it?" one of the giant Californians protested. "We can take care of ourselves."

In an age when soccer fans are barred from each others' countries for murderous behavior, the rugby incident seems relatively tame. But this was 1924, and this was the Olympic Games. French officials were appalled and apologized handsomely. The French press also seemed embarrassed by the fans' unsporting behavior. A sports reporter for *Le Figaro* wrote that he was almost glad the Americans had won, since they were the best players in the world. He added for good measure that he had seen the French team out carousing in Montparnasse the night before the game. The London *Times* saw the incident as

Los Angeles high-school student Lee Barnes soars to victory in the pole vault. The 17-year-old Barnes and silver medalist Glenn Graham of the United States both cleared 12 feet 11 1/2 inches (3.95 meters). Barnes took the gold after beating Graham in a tie-breaking vault.

a reason for ending the Games. In reply, the treasurer of Cambridge University's Athletic Club suggested, no doubt to the bemusement of the nation of Montaigne and Voltaire, "May not the participation of the English speaking peoples in the Olympic Games be regarded in the light of a mission among races whose sense of sportsmanship is more recently evolved?"

It was the players, as usual, who had the right perspective. "The French players were good guys," Charlie Dow offered graciously. "Our guys just ignored the ruckus in the stands."

Mob psychology aside, the reasons behind French distaste for America aren't difficult to understand. In 1924 the United States was the richest nation on earth. The spacious country had room then for wave upon wave of immigration; in the first 10 years of the century alone, it had absorbed six million Europeans. Its ports, cities, and industries were thriving; its vast plains yielded magnificent harvests. America produced half of the planet's oil, copper, wheat, and cotton and a third of its gold and coal.

Wealth on such a scale acquired mythic status, increased by every glimpse. To France came glamorous American movies and big American cars, items available only to the wealthiest in postwar France. "We never had a car—working people didn't in those days," one Frenchwoman's memoir ran, adding wistfully, "but we did have our picture taken beside one when we had gone for an outing in one of the parks in Paris." Cars were not novelties in the United States, though, nor were many of life's other luxuries, and the French knew it. Americans had the biggest and best of everything, the most of everything—all of everything, it sometimes seemed. Americans were easy to envy.

They were also easy to resent. During the war, Europe hemorrhaged blood and money while the United States boomed, safe in its distant, rich, and isolated self-absorption. U.S. exports of war materials and food fueled American prosperity: Between 1914 and 1920, the nation's wealth increased 250 percent. The country maintained a lofty neutrality—Americans should be "too proud to fight" was President Woodrow Wilson's phrase. The U.S. entered the conflict in Europe only during the last 19 months, after Germany had taken to indiscriminate attacks on American shipping. Once in, the Americans had fought well, to be sure, helping to turn the tide of war in favor of the Allies. More than 50,000 U.S. troops died. But the European toll was eight million.

Small wonder, then, that Parisians observed with somewhat jaundiced eyes the American contingent that came to visit in 1924: the 350 athletes (the huge, merciless rugby players) and 100 alternates, the ample array of officials, managers, coaches, their free-spending wives, their provincial ways.

The provincialism was probably forgivable—if not by Parisians, at least by less biased and more clement observers. America was a young country, rich and brash, still more than a little puritanical, far removed in geography and spirit from

Californian Clarence "Bud" Houser hurls the discus for an Olympic record. Equally formidable in the shot put, Houser would win his second gold medal in Paris in that event, achieving a double matched by only one other man in Olympic history, America's Robert Garrett at Athens 1896.

Frenchman L. C. Mascaux created this high-jump medal, not as an award, but as part of his bronze-winning entry in the Olympic arts competition.

Illinois native Harold Osborn clears the bar in the high-jump competition. Osborn would win the gold in the high jump, never missing on a single attempt, then go on to begin the decathlon five days later. He would triumph in that event, too, becoming the only athlete in Olympic history to win both the decathlon and an individual event in track and field.

Old World woes and mores. What Europeans regarded as sophistication, Americans were apt to see as decadence. The two viewpoints were bound to clash. But the Americans, not especially mindful of global politics and economics, probably didn't realize it at the time. In their innocence (their ignorance, Parisians might have said), the U.S. group set out for France expecting only to be coddled and admired. Certainly, they were prepared to be admired.

For the Games, the various American sporting factions had united, more or less, so that all preparations could be handled centrally by the American Olympic Committee. The arrangements were on a scale commensurate with America's size. After regional trials throughout the spring, final trials and selections were completed in June, yielding the best of the best young athletes. On June 16 most of them, along with supporting personnel and guests, set sail from New York on the SS *America*.

Evidently because they feared their athletes would be tempted by the fleshpots of Paris, AOC officials quartered the majority of the team at Rocquencourt. This was a Napoleonic prince's château outside Paris—a scenic enough site, but primitive, by American standards, and a miserable 12-mile ride from the Olympic Stadium. Everybody hated it, and in the American official report—mostly comments from various managers, coaches, and trainers, compiled for the AOC after the Games—many took the chance to complain. The place certainly didn't provide American comforts ("It was awful at Rocquencourt," head field coach Walter M. Christie said). The training facilities were inadequate, the rooms unpleasant, the bathrooms appalling, and the food terrible. ("You could not get an egg cooked the way an athlete wanted it," Christie complained. "We ran out of shredded wheat and cornflakes.") Although it seems hard to believe— this was France, after all—meals were no better at the Olympic Village, where "indifferent food was

prepared indifferently by French cooks, who did not care, and served by waitresses who did not care." Swimming coach Bill Bachrach thought the solution was to hire American cooks and waiters who would feed their athletes "the right American way." "The foreigner," he said, "either doesn't care or doesn't understand, or both, and should not be relied on for this fundamental requirement for American success in the Games."

Most of the carping, however, came from support personnel. The athletes themselves were thrilled to be in the Games, as every athlete is. And as the Americans always had, they came away with the most prizes. But they did not garner gold in every event they expected to win. They did not, for instance, win that most classic of Olympic events, the marathon.

America's hope for the marathon was Clarence de Mar, in many ways a more extreme version of Paavo Nurmi. Born in Ohio in 1888, one of six children of a farmer, de Mar was only eight when his father died. His mother moved the family to Massachusetts and, unable to support all the children, put young Clarence in a charity farm and trade school on Thompson Island in Boston harbor. He graduated in 1903, and this being America, where almost everybody could succeed, went on to the University of Vermont. There he absorbed a professor's theory that every man could be a champion at some sport, and it changed de Mar's life. "I had led a hard and somewhat squelched life since leaving the farm school," he later wrote. "I felt unworthy to associate with people except at work and so I had grown to feel myself as socially inferior. So, more than most young men in life, I felt I would have to do something to really make myself somebody."

Running was that something, and in 1911 de Mar won his first Boston Marathon. What followed was remarkable. The marathon's physician told de Mar that he had a heart murmur and that running would kill him in short order. Convinced by that—and by the fatal heart attack of another marathon runner during a race—the young man stopped running. He spent his peak athletic years in farming, lay preaching, and studying. When the physician himself died of heart disease in 1922, however, de Mar reconsidered the matter. The next year he won his second Boston Marathon. He would win five more—the last when he was 42—and place in the top ten 15 times. He would remain a distance runner until two weeks before his death—from cancer—in 1953.

De Mar's marathon performances made him a Boston favorite, in spite of his irascible, humorless nature. He hated interference in general and invasion of his running space in particular, an attitude that led him to punch bystanders who annoyed him and knock over anyone who got in his way. The man who wanted to be somebody couldn't bear anybody close.

He especially couldn't bear authority, and he was loudly contemptuous of running coaches. In fact, he agreed to run at Paris 1924 only if he would not be responsible to the marathon trainer, a man named Michael Ryan. Officials agreed, and the situation naturally produced some tension on shipboard and in France.

In the Olympic marathon, though, de Mar took only a bronze medal, coming in behind a 41-year-old Finn, Albin Stenroos, and Romeo Bertini of Italy. Stenroos was on the comeback trail at the time. He had set Finnish records in distance racing 17 years earlier and had finished third in the 10,000 meters at the Stockholm Olympics in 1912. But he suffered a severe leg injury in those Games, and in 1917 he retired from running. By 1923 he was back, however, setting a world record in the 20,000 meters. Even so, he seemed a dubious bet to win the ultimate distance race in Paris; he hadn't run a single marathon from 1909 until May of 1924, when he came in second in Finland's Olympic trials. The Olympic victory two months later crowned his career. In the Paris heat wave, his time of 2:41:22.6 was not spectacular, but it was

six minutes ahead of Bertini—and almost seven minutes ahead of de Mar.

The defeat certainly stung de Mar, and Stenroos poured salt into the wound the next year by beating him again, this time on the American's home ground, the Boston Marathon. (Stenroos finished second behind America's Johnny Miles, who set a world record of 2:25:40 in the race. De Mar finished third.) But when de Mar and Stenroos met the next time, in the Philadelphia Marathon in 1926, de Mar ran the Finn—who gave up after 20 miles—into the ground.

De Mar blamed his Olympic failure on coaching interference. Marathon trainer Ryan, getting some of his own back, claimed in the American

Radio commentators for the marathon *(left)* gave fans at Colombes stadium updates of the runners' positions. American fans cheered when it was announced that Clarence de Mar *(No. 210 below)* had moved into the lead after 18 1/2 miles. De Mar would fade near the end of the race and finish third. The winner was 41-year-old Albin Stenroos *(inset)*, whose victory gave Finland a gold-medal sweep of the distance events.

official report that his team made a poor showing because it had been terrified by the descriptions of the debacle in the 10,000-meter cross-country two days before. After the marathon, Ryan said, de Mar had told him that he had "run as fast as he dared to under the conditions." Ryan also furiously recommended that "no runner or runners be given special privileges to pursue his pet ideas regardless of his ability." All was not happy on the U.S. marathon team.

Most of the Americans, though, were both dedicated and convivial. And they performed. Among the sprinters, Jackson Scholz and Charley Paddock were experienced stars. Paddock had won the 100

meters at Antwerp 1920, thus gaining the informal title generally accorded the winner of that particular race, "the fastest man on earth." In Paris, however, Paddock had a fit of nerves the night before the 200-meter race, declaring that he was past his peak and defeat was inevitable. He was somewhat restored by glamorous assistance: pep talks from the movies' most famous couple, Douglas Fairbanks and Mary Pickford (fellow passengers with the team on the *America*), and their friend Maurice Chevalier, who did hilarious imitations of Paavo Nurmi. In the 200 meters, Paddock won the silver, finishing behind his teammate Scholz.

Besides these two, American stars included

Harold Osborn, from the University of Illinois, who won both the decathlon and the high jump, the only man ever to take both events in Olympic competition. Californian Clarence "Bud" Houser won both the discus and the shot put. Among others, there were also American golds in the hammer throw, the 100-meter high hurdles, the 400-meter hurdles, and the pole vault.

Perhaps the most historic field victory, however, was that of William DeHart Hubbard in the long jump. A University of Michigan student, Hubbard became the first black athlete ever to win an individual Olympic gold medal; the silver went to his teammate, Ned Gourdin of Harvard, who was also black. Hubbard's historic triumph was only slightly dimmed by the fact that in the pentathlon, Georgetown's Robert LeGendre had set a world record for the long jump of 25 feet 6 3/16 inches (7.78 meters)—a foot farther than Hubbard had leapt. But it didn't matter at home: Hubbard was a trailblazer.

It may be that the Parisians were unaware of what an achievement this was. African-American culture was the rage in Paris during the 1920s, and life was good for blacks there. The African sculpture that fired Picasso's imagination filled the more advanced galleries. African, West Indian, and American blacks took Paris into the Jazz Age; jazz clubs were packed every night, and composers such as Igor Stravinsky and Erik Satie were publishing piano arrangements of ragtime and using jazz harmonics in their work. The climax of the movement would not be reached until 1925, when the incomparable singer and dancer Josephine Baker arrived from the United States to star at La Revue Negre. Baker accepted only the best. Her costumes (what little there was of them) were designed by Paul Poiret and Elsa Schiaparelli. Her alto saxophonist was Sidney Bechet. Baker enchanted Paris. She was the last word in exotic chic.

Almost certainly, Josephine Baker could hardly even have imagined such heights had she stayed home; when she went to Paris she was escaping the shadow side of American culture. Sixty years after the Civil War, blacks formed a tenth of the American population. Most lived in segregated, impoverished misery. Their very existence was often precarious: Nearly 400,000 had fought in World War I—in segregated regiments, three of which won France's highest wartime honor, the Croix de Guerre. These soldiers returned to a

American Charley Paddock's signature leap at the finish line couldn't propel him to the gold medal in the 200-meter dash. Paddock, 100-meter defending champion and world-record holder lost the 200-meters by less than a foot to teammate Jackson Scholz, who had beaten him over the same distance in 1920.

Visitors to Paris in 1924 headed for the Moulin Rouge *(the "Red Mill" at left)*, a traditional music hall long part of the city's nightlife: It had been immortalized in th 19th century in the paintings and posters of an habitué, Henri de Toulouse-Lautrec. Trendsetters, however, thronged La Revue Negre, a club that featured sensational new American jazz groups like the Claude Hopkins Band *(below)*. The bands, along with Josephine Baker and the irrepressible singer Bricktop—named for her startling red hair—brought African-American culture to an enthusiastic European audience.

DeHart Hubbard, wearing his University of Michigan singlet, takes a break during warm-ups for the long jump.

country where in 1920 alone there were 26 race riots and 76 lynchings. So bloody were the scenes at a five-day riot in St. Louis—Josephine Baker's hometown—that at last a group of blacks and whites began the talks that led to the founding of the National Association for the Advancement of Colored People.

American sport reflected American mores. In the first years of freedom after the Civil War, blacks competed in many sports along with everyone else. All but one of the jockeys at the first Kentucky Derby in 1875, for instance, were black; and blacks competed in professional baseball in the 1880s. But attitudes quickly hardened and walls went up. Blacks were barred from horse racing, as they would be barred from professional boxing (until 1908), football (until the 1940s), and baseball (until 1947). They developed their own leagues. Of course, blacks in college athletics—the pathway to the great prizes of amateur sport—were few and far between.

In this environment, black athletes, like all

The powerful legs of University of Michigan track star William DeHart Hubbard recoil from a landing in the long-jump pit. Hubbard became the first African-American to win an individual gold medal in track and field.

African-Americans, had to be people of astonishing accomplishment and tenacity if they were to survive, let alone prosper. Hubbard was such a person. And as Baron de Coubertin had imagined that disadvantaged amateur athletes would, he had a patron: a white businessman named Len Barringer. Barringer, a University of Michigan alumnus, noticed the splash Hubbard was making in Cincinnati, Ohio, at his high school contests as a sprinter, hurdler, long jumper, and triple jumper. He checked out the boy's scholastic record, which was excellent, and determined to get him into Michigan.

Michigan was no friendlier to blacks than most other universities at the time; coach Fielding H. Yost refused to have any on his football team. When Barringer called, however, Yost agreed to accept Hubbard for the track squad, probably in the interest of improving the university's athletic reputation, then on the rise.

Hubbard lacked tuition money, but Barringer, ever-resourceful, had a plan. The *Cincinnati Enquirer* was holding a subscription contest. The prize was a four-year college scholarship to the student who sold the most subscriptions to the newspaper. Hubbard entered. Barringer got in touch with almost every Michigan alumnus and organization in the country—even the University of Michigan Library subscribed—and DeHart Hubbard won.

And won and won and won. As the *Michigan Daily*—which persisted in referring to Hubbard as "Michigan's dusky athlete"—noted, he produced athletic treasures for the university throughout his career. He habitually won competitions in the 50-yard dash, the 100-yard dash, and the long jump. (The university had to lengthen its jumping pit just for him.) He won before the Olympic Games. He came home from the Games, having reached the ultimate athletic

Georgetown student Robert LeGendre hits the board perfectly as he takes off on a long jump. LeGendre leaped out to a record 25 feet 5 3/4 inches (7.765 meters) during a segment of the pentathlon.

<!-- caption -->A perfect baton pass from Loren Murchison sends Alf Leconey down the track at a world-record pace during the 4 x 100-meter relay. Teams from the Netherlands, Great Britain, and the U.S. broke the previous world standard during heats before the Americans set the mark of 41.0 in the finals.

apex, and he went on winning—for Michigan and for himself. In the last jump of his college career, in the high style of a Nurmi or a de Mar, he officially broke LeGendre's world record by covering 25 feet 10 7/8 inches (7.9 meters).

Then Hubbard returned to Cincinnati and a career of athletics administration, supervising black leagues. Later he was a city housing official. He died in 1976 in Cleveland.

Of all the tales from Paris 1924, possibly the best known today, thanks to the film *Chariots of Fire*, are those of British sprinters Harold Abrahams and Eric Liddell. The film's title, taken from the most beloved and most English of hymns, was an inspired choice. Originally composed by William Blake, the ecstatic lyric came to express the patriotic ideals

and aspirations of 19th-century society, especially in the final stanzas:

> Bring me my Bow of burning gold:
> Bring me my Arrows of desire:
> Bring me my Spear: O Clouds, unfold!
> Bring me my Chariot of Fire.
>
> I will not cease from Mental Fight,
> Nor will my Sword sleep in my hand
> Till we have built Jerusalem
> In England's green and pleasant land.

For most of this century, sport—and especially Olympic sport—reflected the imagination of that society. Great Britain, and every other nation, had always had sports and games, of course: The rulers had their tournaments, their court

Morgan Taylor of the United States takes the lead in the 400-meter hurdles. Taylor would improve the world record in the event by almost 1.5 seconds, but because he knocked down one hurdle, the mark would not be allowed. Finland's Erik Vilén *(second from left)* was awarded the silver medal after judges disqualified American Charles Brookins *(far right)* for running out of his lane.

tennis, their hunting and hawking; the poor had their ball games and village contests. But the traditional sporting ideals known today are the products of the 19th-century Industrial Revolution, the growth of the British Empire, and the rise of a powerful British middle class.

During the 19th century, Britain needed a steady supply of strong, well-educated young men to serve her burgeoning interests. The man most responsible for meeting this need was the brilliant idealist Dr. Thomas Arnold, headmaster of Rugby School from 1828 to 1842. Arnold developed the system that molded England's finest. He believed profoundly in Christianity; he believed in a curriculum based on the classics but including mathematics, modern languages, and modern history; and he believed in the character-shaping virtue of sport. At Rugby he introduced a demanding regimen based on these beliefs, and his system quickly spread to all the schools that nourished the children of the ruling class. Arnold's principles left an indelible imprint on the 19th and early 20th centuries. They were, in fact, an inspiration for a young French aristocrat named Pierre de Coubertin,

who would shape his notion of the Olympic Games around Arnold's ideas.

Under Arnold's influence, such schools as Rugby, Eton, Harrow, and Winchester turned out healthy young men steeped in the ethos of fair play and good sportsmanship. That ethos would travel with them, to England's great universities and well beyond. "To Oxford and Cambridge went the graduates of the public schools," sports historian Allen Guttmann has noted. "From Oxford and Cambridge, the energetic British soldier, civil servant or businessman went forth to Vancouver, Madras, Cape Town or Melbourne. And brought with him the marvels of modern sports." One result of such evangelism was the appearance of amateur athletic associations in the first five industrial nations—Great Britain, the United States, France, Germany, and Sweden. In each country, associations for swimming, bicycling, rowing, tennis, and other sports formed in the 40 years preceding 1900. In every case, Britain's association appeared first.

Arnold's influence was also reflected in the careers of men such as Harold Abrahams and Eric

Liddell. Both were products of the British system. Each, however, brought his own qualities to it. Their approaches to athletics and their lives are a study in contrasts.

Abrahams was born in 1899 in Bedford, the youngest of six children of a Lithuanian Jew who, like thousands of his fellows, had come to England in the 19th century to escape Eastern European poverty and pogroms. A driven, domineering man, the elder Abrahams made a fortune as a financier. He reared his children in luxury, but with discipline. They were bright, competitive, high achievers: The father pressed them to succeed, and they usually did. Two of the older brothers were athletes. One, Sidney, competed (although he didn't win) in the Olympic long jump at Athens 1906 and Stockholm 1912. When younger brother Harold began to show athletic promise, his older brothers pushed him; when he went away to Repton, then a second-division public school (it was unlikely that a Jew would have been admitted to Eton or Harrow in those days), he pushed himself. He made a name as a runner and jumper at the public school championships.

In 1919, as his brothers and sisters had done, Abrahams entered Cambridge University to study law. His college was Gonville and Caius (usually just given as Caius, the Latinized version of Keys, the last name of one of its founders). Although he didn't run around the college court in a race against the clock, as cinematic art would have it, Abrahams quickly won his athletic blue both as runner and jumper. In English intercollegiate events, he won just about every prize possible. He ran the 100 yards (the British races were run in yards, not meters) in 10 seconds. He set a record for the British long jump—24 feet 2 1/2 inches—that would not be broken until 1956. He was an obvious candidate for Britain's 1920 Olympic track team. He wasn't in the class of runners like Charley Paddock or Jackson Scholz yet, and he didn't shine. He lost in a

quarterfinal heat. But Abrahams would make sure he shone at the next Games.

Chariots of Fire asserts that Abrahams credited Cambridge anti-Semitism for his athletic drive; his friends and family deny it, as does Caius College, which was so offended by the film's emphasis on the subject that it refused to cooperate with the project. Nevertheless, there is probably at least some truth to the story: A strong vein of anti-Semitism ran through the British establishment in the 1920s. Unless a young man's family was as fabulously wealthy as the Rothschilds or the Sassoons, he was apt to feel it, at least subtly. Abrahams' family, however, believed that Harold strove because it was in his nature to strive.

It remains arguable whether Cambridge University and the British Olympic Committee were put off by Abrahams' Jewishness. Beyond question, however, they disapproved of his hiring a professional coach to direct his training. Gentlemen, after all, didn't do such things.

The coach in question was Sam Mussabini, himself no gentleman by any British definition. Half Arab, half French, Mussabini was an expert on cycling and billiards as well as running. He had been around for a while: He had coached South African runner Reginald Hill to victory in the Olympic 100 meters at London 1908. He had also worked the professional circuit. This didn't go down well at all. As one of Abrahams' friends—who claimed to admire his efforts—said, it was out of keeping with the spirit of the time. "Harold was almost professional," he observed, "although obviously not in the sense of getting any remuneration."

"Almost professional" was no compliment. A gentleman sportsman eschewed professionalism in any form. Sport was a social institution that helped define the British middle classes, and they zealously guarded its amateur character. Sport should be played for itself alone. Training professionally was the kind of thing the lower orders did—that, and taking money. The attitude was

Sprinters poise for the start of the 100-meter finals. Prognosticators gave Harold Abrahams *(third from left)* an outside shot at a bronze medal. The favorites were Americans Jackson Scholz *(second from right)* and defending champion Charley Paddock *(far right)*.

fueled by class prejudice as much as by idealism. (As late as 1960, British writers were capable of arguing that "the average workman has no idea of sport for its own sake.")

Plebeian or not, the hiring of Sam Mussabini made Harold Abrahams into a spectacular sprinter. Maintaining that "the action of the arms controlled the poise of the body and the action of the legs," Mussabini meticulously taught Abrahams the mechanics of running. The coach knew that a runner attains maximum power by putting the optimum number of strides into a given distance, and he taught the youth to control his stride. He had Abrahams use a length of string to make a mark on the track where his first step would land. Each subsequent step was mapped by pieces of paper set out by Mussabini at measured distances; Abrahams was supposed to spear them with his spikes as he sprinted. Eventually, Abrahams knew exactly how many strides he would use to cover any given distance. He also knew, from hours of supervised practice and repetition, how to reach top speed in minimum time, and how to drop forward at the race's finish so that his torso would reach the tape millimeters before his legs.

Abrahams might have shown what he had learned in the 1923 British Amateur Athletic Association championships, but he was sick at the time. The star of the championships was

the Scot Eric Liddell, who won both the 100- and 200-yard sprints (the 100 in 9.7 seconds). The next week, in Great Britain's Triangular Contest among England, Scotland, and Ireland, Liddell pulled off what connoisseurs would call the greatest athletic feat they had ever seen: Knocked off the track at the start of the 440-yard race, he hesitated, thinking himself disqualified. By the time he realized he was still in, he was 20 yards behind the field. But Liddell tore after the others as if he heard the hounds of heaven at his back. He won the race by two yards. There was little doubt that he would be an Olympic speed champion.

It would be hard to find a man more different from Abrahams than Eric Liddell. The son of a devout and loving family of Scottish Congregationalist missionaries, he was born in

A terrific start, coupled with the Mussabini lean, gave Abrahams the 100-meter title he coveted.

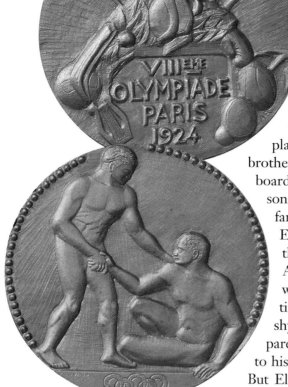

Medals for the VIII Olympiad were designed by André Rivaud, a student at the Beaux Arts School in Paris. The front gives the numbered Olympiad and year of the Games, surrounded by pieces of sports equipment. The back depicts a triumphant athlete from ancient times helping a fallen rival—a symbol of good sportsmanship.

Tientsin, China, in 1902. His parents returned to Scotland on furlough in 1907 and the following year placed Eric and his older brother in Eltham College, a boarding school for the sons of missionaries, not far from Greenwich in England. The parents then went back to their Asian mission. Eric was only six at the time. He was small and shy and he missed his parents badly. He clung to his brother.

But Eltham's headmaster believed passionately in Dr. Arnold's theories: Fresh air and sports gave a boy a chance to shine; they built courage; they taught team spirit. As this sensible philosophy did with most boys, it worked with Eric Liddell. He was no more than a competent student, but he was a natural athlete, and he did shine— on the track, in the field, and at rugby, the sport he truly loved. He was fast. "I don't think much of the lessons," he told his sister. "But I can run."

This truth was noted soon after Liddell entered Edinburgh University in the autumn of 1920 to study science. Within a few months, he had been recruited for the Edinburgh University Athletic Club. It was all very casual, in classic amateur style. A hardworking student, Liddell trained when he had time (on a dog-racing track, with whippets barking on the sidelines). He played rugby, too, but running was his natural sport. Within a year he dominated sprinting in university matches. He won everything—100 yards, 220, 440, year after year. He gave so many trophy cups, watches, dishes, and vases to his mother and

younger sister (they had returned to Edinburgh in 1920) that the objects had to be stowed under the beds. He was the most famous athlete in Scotland.

Among the things Liddell was famous for was his running style, very unorthodox and very much his own. Even by the most informal standards it was inefficient, and by Mussabini's lights it was ludicrous. Liddell ran like an animated windmill. His arms flailed in every direction. His knees flew high into the air. He wobbled. And in the exultation running brought him, he threw his head far back and ran gazing at the clouds. He didn't even look where he was going. He ran as if celestial trumpets were summoning him from the other side, and indeed, commentators from that day to this have assumed that his phenomenal speed—so clearly unaided by the mechanics of his running—must have been inspired by his faith. Liddell, a quiet and diffident man, was profoundly imbued with the Christian beliefs of his fathers. His faith would lead him to become a missionary, as his father and brother were. It would lead him to his death. He dedicated himself to the church, with his whole heart and apparently without question.

As everyone who knew him invariably attested, Liddell's religion was of a loving and clement kind; he was never rigid or sanctimonious. Outside his work, he rarely drew attention to his faith. Christianity was simply part of the fabric of his character, like his charm, his humor, his practicality, his bravery, his kindness. And his chivalry in competition. He was a man who shook hands all around before a match and wished everyone luck. He was much loved. He was by all accounts that rare thing, a truly good man.

Because this was so, people who knew him were not surprised when Liddell refused to run the 100-meter race at the 1924 Olympic Games. The schedules, issued six months before the event (not at the last instant, as the film would have it) revealed that the heats for the 100 meters were set for Sunday, July 6, and the Scot's church forbade him to run on the Sabbath. "Liddell was the last person to make a song and dance about that sort of thing," one of his friends would recall years later. "He just said, 'I'm not running on a Sunday'—and that was that. And he would have been very upset if anything much had been made of it at the time."

British athletic officials did make something of it, however. As anyone who understood running knew, Liddell was, in effect, surrendering a much-desired gold medal. He was ceding, without a fight, a very probable victory in the most prestigious race in the world. Eventually, however, the officials accepted the decision and agreed that Liddell would run the 200 and 400 meters instead. He began to train.

The press was intemperate about the affair. There were angry remarks about national honor. Liddell was called a traitor in print. The criticism stung, and, it was said, he had doubts about his decision up until the last minute. Nevertheless, Sunday, July 6, found him preaching at the Scottish Kirk in Paris, while Abrahams ran the 100-meter heats.

Abrahams was Britain's hope now, and he was a faint one, even to himself. He had been trained by Mussabini, but he would be running against Charley Paddock, the defending champion, as well as Jackson Scholz and another American, Loren Murchison. Both Scholz and Murchison had been among the finalists at Antwerp 1920.

On Monday, though, with Liddell cheering him on and Mussabini's now-famous advice ("Only think of two things—the report

of the pistol and the tape. When you hear the one, just run like hell until you break the other") echoing in his ears, Abrahams ran the race of his life. He burst out of the starting holes to hit the tape in 10.6 seconds, tying Paddock's Olympic record and beating Paddock himself. It was faster than Abrahams had ever run, or would ever run again. The performance surprised everyone. Years later, Jackson Scholz, who came in second, would be asked whether he remembered the man he followed to the tape that day in Paris. Scholz grinned. "I remember his ass," he said.

Probably tired, Abrahams placed an undistinguished sixth in the 200 meters on Wednesday, July 9. He was well behind Scholz, Paddock, and Liddell (who finished in that order, Liddell running his first race and taking the bronze). But any disappointment Abrahams may have felt at his poor showing in the 200-meter event was doubtless salved by the prestigious gold he had already won in the fastest race of all. He was the first European ever to triumph in the 100 meters, and he remained the only Briton to do it until Scotland's Allan Wells won at Moscow 1980. Now it was Liddell's turn to run his 400 meters, the connoisseur's race that requires the speed of a sprinter and the stamina of a middle-distance runner. It demands pacing and invincible will. Liddell, however, believed that by a curious irony, it was turning out to be his natural race. He was becoming more comfortable with the longer distance than he had been with the 100 meters, the race he had once

All participants at the Paris Games received this commemorative medal. A champion is crowned on one side; the other side bears an inscription.

51

Tape measure in hand, England's Harold Abrahams maps out his race. Measured paces, dictated by his controversial professional coach, were the key to Abrahams' speed in the 100-meter dash.

deemed his forte. His competitors, featuring America's Horatio Fitch and England's Guy Butler, were covering the distance in around 48 seconds. Before the Olympics, Liddell had never run it in less than 49, but in his three heats, on Thursday and Friday morning, he had gradually decreased his time to 48.2.

Nevertheless, there were mixed omens on the day of the race. Liddell drew the outside lane, dreaded by all runners because in the staggered start, the outside man can't see his opposition. On the other hand, the Scot was bolstered by much loving support. There was a note, paraphrasing I Samuel 2:30: "In the old book it says, 'He that honours me I will honour.'" The note was delivered on the morning of the race. It had been signed by his masseur and by all his teammates. There was also the

band of the 2nd Queen's Own Cameron Highlanders, brought to Paris as the British musicians for the Games. The bandsmen happened to be standing at trackside just before the 400 began, and on impulse they decided to give Liddell a lift. Electrifying the audience, they marched around the track, kilts swinging and pipes wailing that most Scottish of tunes, "The Campbells Are Coming."

Whether moved by the Bible or the music, Liddell ran his race like a man inspired. When the gun went off, he shot out as if he were running a dash, covering the first 200 meters in 22.2 seconds—a 200-meter race time, and, it seemed, an impossible pace to sustain. Two of his opponents fell, trying to keep up, but Fitch and Butler stayed with him, two meters behind. Then, in the last seconds, Liddell did the unheard of: In

Liddell breasts the tape at the finish of the 400-meter dash. Even though he ran the first half of the race 0.3 of a second shy of his 200-meter time, Liddell easily held off the competition, America's Horatio Fitch (second from left) and Great Britain's Guy Butler (second from right), to take the gold medal.

Eric Liddell displays his bizarre but unbeatable running technique in the early stages of the 400-meter dash. Actor Ian Charleson, who portrayed Liddell with unnerving accuracy in the 1981 film *Chariots of Fire*, once said the hardest part of the role was learning to run as badly as the gold medalist.

his ecstatic, flailing, head-back style, he increased his lead from two to five meters. He won in 47.6 seconds, an Olympic record.

What happened afterward to the two winners was as different as what had gone before—and as in character. Harold Abrahams never ran in another Olympic Games. In 1925, on a long jump in a minor contest, he tore virtually every muscle and nerve in one leg; he said later that he heard them ripping like a piece of sailcloth. His athletic career was over. He would walk with a limp for the rest of his life.

He was philosophical about this disaster. Perhaps he knew, as Jackson Scholz believed, that the 10 seconds of the 100-meter race were the apex of a runner's life. He went on to a fine legal career, but the memory of Paris 1924 propelled him into sports reporting and administration as a second vocation. Abrahams was the track and field correspondent of the *Times* of London for almost 40 years, and he dominated the BBC sports department for almost as long. He married a light-opera singer (whom he met in 1935) and they led the comfortable and civilized life of the British Establishment.

Characteristically, though, Abrahams always seemed to rouse a certain amount of controversy. His family remembered him as a loyal and kindhearted man—if a trifle eccentric. (He always wore three stopwatches and timed every action of his day.) But his critics described him as imperious and rigid, and intensely class-conscious. A poacher turned gamekeeper, he regarded coaches as his social inferiors and tried to bar their progress in track and field. Members of the press questioned his dual role in sports administration and in reportage—and resented his iron control over British sports reporting. No one, however, denied his love of sport, or his voluminous knowledge, or his dedication—or the glory of his 1924 victory.

Liddell returned to Edinburgh a hero—his Edinburgh colleagues garlanded him with olive leaves and carried him shoulder-high through the city streets. He was pleased, of course, but not immoderately so: Earthly glory had never been his motive or his goal.

He spent his last year in Scotland studying divinity, and in 1925 he left as a missionary to join his brother in China. He taught science to Chinese students in Tientsin for 12 years, and although he was interested in athletics and occasionally raced, he made little of it. He fell in love with the 17-year-old daughter of Canadian missionaries, and in 1932 he married her. They would have three daughters. When China descended into internal chaos and lay open to Japanese invasion in the late 1930s, Liddell sent his family to Canada for safety. He stayed with his mission in the remote wastes of the Great Plain of China. In 1943, with other Europeans, he was imprisoned in a Japanese internment camp. He died in great privation there, of a brain tumor, in 1945. Scotland went into national mourning. The report in the *Glasgow Evening News* said, and rightly, "Scotland has lost a son who did her proud every hour of his life."

Of the two athletes, Harold Abrahams, no matter how conservative, seems the more modern. Even his conflicts have a contemporary ring.

Eric Liddell, however, seems touched by the very spirit of Olympia. In the wild ecstasy of his running, in his joy at his own sheer speed, he expressed the exultant human mastery that makes the Games what they are. People who watch them catch an echo of the joy. But the athlete—the runner speeding from the mark, the vaulter releasing the pole at the height of its spring, the diver or the skier in the freedom of his flight—is the one who lives within that incandescent moment, when the clouds of self unfold before him and his frail frame alone becomes the chariot of fire.

THE GOLDEN DAYS

Among the settings for the Paris 1924 Games, the Stade Nautique des Tourelles was probably the most spectacular, both in location and design. The pool was built in the 20th Arrondissement, a quarter formed in the 1860s when the expanding city absorbed outlying hill villages to the east. Traces of those villages still remained, in narrow, cobbled streets and hillside stairs, in small stone houses and tiny gardens, and in street names such as Amandiers, Muriers, and Pruniers, relics of the almond, mulberry, and plum orchards that once had grown there. But the little villages themselves—Belleville, Menilmontant, Charonne—were disappearing into the rich fabric of Paris.

The 20th Arrondissement was as international as the Games. Within it were kosher butcher shops run by Jews from Eastern Europe and Tunisia, Italian delicatessens, Chinese grocery stores, Moroccan spice stands. The weekly street markets echoed with exotic harmonies. Through the crowds wandered chic Vietnamese from French Indochina, West Africans in bright turbans, dark-eyed Arabs in the burnooses of the desert. The people's politics tended to be Communist, that most modern of philosophies. Residents of the 20th Arrondissement had a long tradition of working-class radicalism. The short-lived Paris Commune had made its last stand behind street barricades here in 1871, and no one forgot it: Along with more famous permanent Parisians, from Heloise and Abelard to Oscar Wilde and, more recently, Amedeo Modigliani, the Communards had a monument in Père Lachaise Cemetery at the edge of the quarter.

The swimming stadium completed here in 1923 was, like the neighborhood, a synthesis of old and new, native and foreign. It lay high on a hill, near the boulevards—called after Napoleon's marshals—that encircled the city; indeed, the name of Tourelles itself recalled an even earlier period: The word, meaning "turrets," commemorated a towered building that had once stood within the long-gone

Johnny Weissmuller, June 2, 1904-January 20, 1984. Olympic Gold Medalist, 1924, 1928

castle of Menilmontant. The Tourelles complex, designed by French architects and engineers working to international standards, was the first true swimming stadium the Games had ever had. As recently as 1920, Olympians had competed in the remains of Antwerp's city moat, which was so cold that some of the swimmers were dragged out suffering from hypothermia and so murky that divers lost their sense of direction under the water.

In Paris, however, there was an 18-by-50-meter steel basin surrounded by a concrete deck and by high-rising grandstands with seats for 10,000 people. The water was filtered and heated; the lanes were divided by markers. Swimmers and divers, most of them all too accustomed to conditions not much better than Antwerp's, were delighted. The only criticism anybody had was that the diving boards and platforms were sited on a long edge of the pool, so that competitors dived into the width of the water rather than the length. The resulting illusion, especially from the 10-meter platform, was of diving directly into the grandstand opposite. On the other hand, one diver said, when you were on the platform you had a spectacular view over the rooftops and spires of Paris to the city's monumental heart.

The pool was a sports milestone, as was the competition it harbored. Setting record after record, the Olympic swimmers in Paris were pioneers pointing the way to what their sport might become. Chief among them was the affable Johnny Weissmuller. Big, strong, and handsome, Weissmuller quickly became an international idol, leading a remarkable team of Americans. These included the Hawaiian Duke Paoa Kahanamoku, already a legend, and his brother Sam; there were also 18 young women, among them Gertrude Ederle, who would shortly become a legend in her own right as the first woman to swim the English Channel. Although they would take 11 of 15 gold medals, the Americans faced formidable and colorful competition,

especially from Sweden and Australia, and—in water polo—from their French hosts.

Perhaps because even competitive swimming frees the body from gravity and gives the heart ease, these swimmers were a good-natured, lively lot. Many remained lifelong friends, despite cultural barriers and years of competition. They were popular with the crowds, too. Parisians flocked to see them conquer the water in the heat of that long-ago July.

This aura of amity didn't necessarily prevail, however, among the athletes, judges, and spectators at other events. There were scenes in some competitions to rival the rugby riot that had preceded the Games. Among the racewalkers, ludicrous misunderstandings seemed endemic. Bad-tempered incidents enlivened the fencing competitions, too. And when it came to boxing, as might be expected, the conflicts were savage; in fact, fights among the fans tended to obscure the quality of the battles in the ring.

Most of the conflicts—as at any Games—were ignited by high-strung personalities and fueled by national pride. Sometimes it appeared that World War I was being fought again on the playing grounds of Paris. Moreover, the press helped keep emotions simmering. Journalists knew that sport provided good stories—stories with heroes and villains and plenty of drama. International competition—games as war—added another interesting layer.

Tennis—especially women's tennis—had everything the sportswriters required. The game demanded not only skill but also intelligence and flair. It was glamorous and elegant. It already had an international circuit and international stars. In 1924 these included two women who had changed the nature of women's tennis. Each had a distinctive style; each was a heroine in her own country. Even better, one was French—Suzanne Lenglen, possibly the greatest woman tennis player who ever lived. Lenglen, a glittering neurotic, was every inch the prima donna. On the

POSTMARKED PARIS

Stamps became a regular part of the Olympic Games at Paris 1924. Twice before, at Athens 1896 and Antwerp 1920, governments had issued Olympic stamps to help raise funds. Paris was different: The Games' organizers had enough money; they wanted the stamps as promotional tools. Glad to oblige, France's postmaster printed 135 million copies of four commemorative issues *(left, at corners)*. Athletes bought some 50,000 of them as souvenirs. Contributing to the high demand was the novelty of the first-ever Olympic Village post office, which operated from May 15 through July 28. The Games made more postal history when Uruguay, delighted with its soccer team's victory in the Olympic tournament at Paris, created a special edition of three stamps *(left, center)*. Available for only three days beginning on August 29, 1924, these were the first Olympic-related stamps ever issued by a non-host country.

court she wore brief, floating silks designed especially for her; off court she covered them with voluminous ermine coats. Her competition was the American Helen Wills, a beautiful Californian. Cold, humorless, determinedly prim, Wills clung to proper white cotton and played a powerful, hard-smashing game. The Paris Games—the last for 60 years to include tennis—seemed the perfect place for them to meet at last. The press had

been suggesting it for months. Lenglen and Wills made good copy, and good copy sold newspapers and newsreels and radio air time.

The women tennis stars created profit, and the profit sports could bring was already obvious in 1924. It wasn't just the newspapers that the new media conglomerates could sell: Amateur athletic associations and clubs reaped publicity and gate receipts from their nurseries of athletes.

That was one reason for the fierce control of those athletes' amateur status—and for the various unofficial financial incentives the stars received. When and if an athlete turned professional—when he performed openly for pay—he could become a gold mine, not only to himself but to the publishers who published his story, the companies whose products he endorsed, and most of all to the impresarios who arranged his athletic exhibitions. Sports was becoming entertainment. That much was obvious from the career of Johnny Weissmuller.

Weissmuller's great good fortune was that he was ready for swimming just when the sport was ready for an athlete of his caliber. Before his day, in fact, swimming was hardly a sport at all.

Japan held swimming contests as early as the first century BC, and swimming was part of ancient Greek and Roman military training. But swimming as an athletic pursuit went into general decline in the West during the Middle Ages and Renaissance because of a sensible fear of waterborne infection. By the late 18th century, physicians were prescribing ocean swimming, but what they had in mind was a quick dip in the English Channel or the North Sea, made by people wearing up to 20 pounds of woolen clothing for modesty and clinging to anchored ropes for safety. February was said to be the healthiest month for this activity.

Only with the 19th-century athletic revival did interest in swimming for sport appear in Europe. There were British competitions as early as the 1840s, but the athletes were slow and the contests dull to watch. Most people swam stately breaststrokes or sidestrokes, and even though crawl-like techniques were imported to Europe during the next decades, all the freestyle competitors in the first modern Games, Athens 1896, swam on their sides.

Four years later, swimmers were all using some version of the crawl, said variously to have originated in South Africa, South America, or Polynesia. But the technique needed streamlining before it would become the swift, water-cleaving stroke of modern competition. It also needed someone to show how perfectly economical and beautiful it could be.

Weissmuller would be that person. Planing high across the water with his powerful long arms, riding his own bow wave, steadying himself with a six-beat flutter kick, he brought drama to the sport. He also brought a personal charm that enlivened every meet he swam in; as sportswriter Paul Gallico put it, "through all this top-flight competition, he was being himself—a character, light-hearted, gay, irresponsible, fun-loving, clowning, overflowing with that mysterious substance we call star quality."

Weissmuller's renown could hardly have been predicted from his beginnings. Born in 1904, the son of immigrant Austrians, he was reared on the meaner streets of North Chicago, in a neighborhood of small brick row houses and ethnic gangs. His father, a failed saloon keeper and a heavy drinker, regularly beat his wife and two sons. The elder Weissmuller died when Johnny was only a boy. The mother, a restaurant cook, held the family together, and Johnny helped out as an errand boy and then as a bellhop and elevator operator at the Chicago Plaza Hotel. He had to drop out of school. Enduring those early, angry years of withering poverty, he vowed that someday life would be different. "I made up my mind," he said years later, "to fight myself out any way I could."

Oddly enough, considering where he lived, swimming armed him for the fight. Johnny was a spindly child, and when he was eight, his mother consulted a physician about the boy's health. Following the doctor's advice, she bought her son a pair of water wings and introduced him to Lake Michigan. He took to the water like a dolphin. He was a natural.

An on-site post office was a popular feature at Paris' primitive Olympic Village. The village was designed for day use only. Overnight quarters for athletes wouldn't become part of the Olympic scene until 1932 at Los Angeles. Most of America's Olympians stayed at a château called Rocquencourt (below), where the decor was posh even if the plumbing was not. The château was preferable to the tent city near Colombes where some 80 U.S. team members had to stay because Rocquencourt was overcrowded.

Swim coach Bill Bachrach *(center)* clowns with Johnny Weissmuller *(left)* and Arne Borg, two of his star pupils from the Illinois Athletic Club.

BACHRACH AND THE IAC

Even if he hadn't produced more swimming champions than any other coach of his era, Bill Bachrach would have been an unusual man. For one thing, he looked odd. He weighed over 300 pounds and had a mouthful of gold teeth that he often accessorized with a cigar. As a youth Bachrach had aspired to become a champion swimmer himself, but he wasn't much of an athlete. His competitive career began and ended with one race in 1897. He finished last. Still, swimming remained his passion, and he decided to take up coaching. The wisdom of that decision was clear by 1908, when Michael McDermott, a Bachrach swimmer at the Chicago YMCA, set the first of a flurry of world records. Impressed, the Illinois Athletic Club (IAC), a competing Chicago-area club, hired Bachrach away in 1912. The coach's motivational skills and his stroke techniques—tailored to each individual athlete—turned the IAC into a national swimming power. Its greatest years were 1914, when its swimmers won every men's event in the AAU championships, and 1924, when it finished the U.S. swimming season undefeated. Predictably, the American Olympic Association picked Bachrach to coach the 1924 U.S. Olympic swim team. The American medal harvest in Paris came in no small part from his own IAC charges: Johnny Weissmuller, Ethel Lackie, and Sybil Bauer. (Arne Borg was also a club member but swam for Sweden.) Among them, Weissmuller, Lackie, and Bauer won six gold medals, two silvers, and a bronze. By any standard, Bachrach was one of the world's greatest swimming coaches: The man who couldn't swim fast developed six Olympic gold medalists and 120 national champions who could.

He lacked technique and style, though: He swam for fun. It was not until the autumn of 1920, when he was 16, that Weissmuller became the protégé of the legendary Bill Bachrach, the 350-pound, cigar-smoking swimming coach of America's 1920 Olympic team. Bachrach was then coaching swimmers at the famed Illinois Athletic Club.

In those days, American athletes had only two routes to top training and amateur competition: universities, for those who could afford to go, and wealthy organizations such as the Los Angeles, Chicago, Illinois, Detroit, or New York athletic clubs. The universities weren't supposed to recruit athletes, but there were no restrictions on the clubs. Young sportsmen who could win championships wearing club colors attracted publicity, prestige, and paying members, and the clubs actively sought promising youths—even poor ones—who received free memberships and training from the best instructors money could buy. Bachrach was such an instructor, and he was always on the lookout for talent.

Stories vary as to how the famous coach first met the poor kid from Cleveland Avenue. But however it happened, Bachrach saw something promising in Johnny Weissmuller's tryout in the club pool. It wasn't his style that created the impression: That was a slow, clumsy, energy-wasting disaster. But the youngster stood a slender 6 feet 3 1/2 inches tall; he had broad shoulders, narrow hips, and very long legs—a perfect swimmer's body. Bachrach took him on, with the promise to make him a champion, if the boy would only follow orders.

In long hours of practice, from October 1920 to August 1921, Bachrach restructured Weissmuller's swimming. The coach taught his student an efficient pull-and-push arm stroke and a powerful kick from the hip. He taught the constant, regular breathing that keeps oxygen flowing to the muscles—most swimmers breathed when they felt like it—and he taught the art of inhaling on alternate sides, the better to watch out for rivals. He taught racing starts and perfect racing turns with strong push-offs. (Swimmers back then touched the wall, turned horizontally, and pushed off with their feet; the flip turn in its modern form didn't appear until the 1960s.) Most notably, Bachrach trained Weissmuller to produce the speed that pushed a bow wave up ahead of him, and to arch his back so that he rode the wave like a hydroplane.

The coach kept his protégé out of competition all this time. Late in 1921, though, Weissmuller was ready to enter the AAU championships representing the club. It was, to put it mildly, an auspicious debut: He won four races and set four national records. By 1923 he was a star. At the AAU's indoor meet that year he won the 50-, 100-, 220-, and 500-yard races and anchored the club's relay team. Then he swam the 100-yard backstroke, breaking the world record by 6.8 seconds.

All during these years, as Bachrach trained the boy, he also helped support him. Betting was the technique: Bachrach would wager a businessman that Weissmuller would beat a given swimming record in the club pool. When Weissmuller did it, the coach took payment in whatever goods the man dealt in—clothing or food, for example—and passed them on. He kept his swimmer an amateur; at the same time, he kept him from starving.

It was obvious that Johnny Weissmuller was heading for international championship, although nobody knew how big a champion he would be. He qualified easily in the June Olympic trials and sailed aboard the SS *America* with the rest of the 66-person team of swimmers and support personnel. The squad included "the greatest swimming and water polo teams ever assembled in the history of American swimming," according to its proud manager, John Taylor. Bill Bachrach was the men's head coach.

Discipline was strict, both on shipboard and in Paris. On the *America*, the swimmers worked out in a small canvas tank, either swimming in place

Johnny Weissmuller *(top)*
stretches his rangy frame into a
dive at the start of the 400-
meter freestyle, but Swedish
champion Arne Borg *(second
from top)* breaks the water first.
The two swapped the lead three
times over the first 300 meters
of the race.

suspended by ropes or alternating arm and leg exercises using inflated tires. In Paris most of the team stayed at Rocquencourt, although overcrowding mandated that some 80 of the men had to stay at a tent village near Colombes stadium. They were so closely supervised there that they called it "the Boy Scout Camp." Still, no one tried to sneak out: Rumor had it that the Olympic officials had spies in the bars and cafés.

The reward for hard work and seclusion came on July 19 with Weissmuller's first race, the 400-meter freestyle. This was a race of masters. Besides Weissmuller, there was Sweden's legendary

bad boy, Arne Borg. Borg loved a good time, he trained when he felt like it, and he swam in whatever style suited his mood—arms only or with two-, four-, or six-beat kicks. He still managed to set 30 individual world records between 1921 and 1929, and the Swedes loved him. When he was briefly imprisoned for taking a holiday in Spain rather than answering his draft call, his fans sent so much food to his cell that he gained 17 pounds. Here was a man after Weissmuller's own heart, and in fact the two—along with Borg's twin brother Åke, also a formidable swimmer and also competing in the 400 meters—became good

Weissmuller pulls away in the last 20 meters to touch the wall first. Borg, previously unbeaten in the event, finished second.

A happy winner of the 1,500-meter freestyle, Australia's Andrew "Boy" Charlton had already taken a bronze in the 400 meters and would win a silver as a member of the 4 x 200-meter relay team.

friends. They did a lot of clowning around during the heats for this race, to the delight of the crowd and the exasperation of officials.

Up from Australia came 17-year-old Andrew Charlton, known as "Boy" because of his youth. He and Arne Borg already knew each other: The year before, they had had a spectacular series of contests in Sydney harbor. They were good-natured about their competitions. When Charlton beat the Swede in the 440-yard race in Sydney, the irrepressible Borg rowed him in a dinghy the length of the course, shouting to the crowd, "Charlton is a champion. I ask you to cheer the champion." Then he said he would beat the boy another time, perhaps at the Olympic Games.

They had already raced once in these Games, and Charlton had beaten Borg to the gold in the 1,500-meter freestyle—by 40 meters, in a world-record time of 20:6.6. This was despite the fact

that it was the youth's first Olympic race and his first time competing in a pool with lane markers, which caused him some anxiety. A further handicap was that Boy had just lost his trainer and mentor, and in the most bizarre way: A shell-shocked survivor of World War I, the man had thrown himself into the sea during the Australians' voyage to Paris; he was sent home in the care of nurses and guards.

The world's best swimmers were in their prime in 1924. They seemed to embody Pierre de Coubertin's dreams of fit and noble youth—and the sparkle of Paris as it was then. As they lined up for the start—Weissmuller ambling over last, as usual—Charlton said, "I hope the best of us wins." "I hope we all win," Weissmuller replied cheerfully.

They didn't all win, of course, but they swam a thrilling race, with Weissmuller and Arne Borg no more than a meter and a half apart at any time, and Charlton just behind. Borg led by inches at 100 meters, Weissmuller at the halfway mark, Borg at 300 meters. Just 20 meters before the end, Weissmuller poured on extra power. He won in 5:4.2, an Olympic record. The effort was so exhausting that Weissmuller had to be helped from the pool; Arne Borg, who took the silver, collapsed. Boy Charlton finished third, but at least he was still standing after the ordeal.

Two days later, Arne Borg and Weissmuller met again in the finals of the 100-meter freestyle. This time they also faced the defending champion, Duke Paoa Kahanamoku, and his brother Sam, Hawaiian men who had begun swimming almost as soon as they could walk and who spent much of every day in the water. Weissmuller feared they might swim a team race against him—one brother setting a fast pace to tire him so that the other could take the gold—but this wasn't that kind of meet. Just before the start, Duke Kahanamoku smiled and said, "Johnny, good luck. The most

important thing in this race is to get the American flag up there three times. Let's do it." It was a fine gesture from an aging champion—Kahanamoku was 34 at the time—to his successor: Weissmuller had been the first person to swim 100 meters in less than a minute and he still held the world record, 57.4 seconds, which would last for 10 years. In this race, he had a swift start and won in 59 seconds, an Olympic record. Kahanamoku and his brother won the silver and the bronze, respectively, to send the three flags up together, as the Hawaiian had hoped.

On the same day, Weissmuller also won a gold medal in the 4 x 200-meter relay and a bronze in water polo. The French water polo team won the gold, to the wild joy of the French fans. In between his events, Weiss-

muller entertained the Parisian audience with a comedy diving exhibition: He executed perfect swan dives, gainers, somersaults, and jackknives from the high platform while a teammate from his athletic club, Harold "Stubby" Kruger, dressed in clown costume, imitated him below, with disastrous results. This kind of thing, along with his perfect swimming and his sheer physical beauty, made Weissmuller the darling of the 1924 Games.

Johnny Weissmuller's athletic career lasted until 1929. When he retired, he held five Olympic gold medals and every world freestyle record from 100 yards to the half mile. He swam in exhibitions throughout Europe and Japan, and wherever he went he was idolized.

But an athlete peaks young; Weissmuller, for

Duke Kahanamoku *(right)* of Hawaii, a two-time gold medalist in the 100-meter freestyle, shakes hands with teammate Johnny Weissmuller. The 19-year-old Weissmuller had just dethroned the 34-year-old champion for the sprint title. Weissmuller would win the 100 again at Amsterdam 1928 along with a relay gold, raising his career Olympic-medal total to five golds and one bronze. The bronze was for America's third-place finish in water polo in 1924.

With towering Art Deco architecture, a big American flag, lavish chorus numbers, and Olympic champions for stars, Billy Rose's Aquacades adds glamor to the 1939 New York World's Fair. Like the similarly staged Ice Capades, the swimming and diving revue did much to cheer Depression-era America—and introduced the sport to millions.

instance, was only 25 when he faced the prospect of watching his glory fade while the rest of his life stretched out ahead. For some champions—those like Harold Abrahams or Eric Liddell—the problem is no more than mild regret. Athletics play only a part in their lives, and the Olympic Games are just a glorious interlude. But people like Johnny Weissmuller, uneducated and untrained for anything but their sport, confront a void. This being so, Olympic history is littered with tragedies.

But Weissmuller wasn't among them. Insouciant as always, he followed his luck, which was considerable. Bachrach found him his first job, as a traveling bathing-suit representative and model. He earned $500 a week for this—extra-

ordinary money during the 1930s. Then he discovered—as many attractive athletes did—the joys of show business.

For retired Olympic swimmers in those days, show business most often meant Billy Rose's Aquacades. These, the brainchild of the most flamboyant of promoters, were grandiose spectacles attached to expositions and world's fairs, shows that featured mammoth pools with floating stages, high-diving platforms, curtains of spouting water, orchestras, choirs, and waterborne casts of hundreds. There were glittering chorus lines of synchronized swimmers (known as Aquabelles and Aquaboys) and every Olympic champion Rose could entice into performing his star numbers. Among

them were Duke Kahanamoku and Johnny Weissmuller. Weissmuller's specialty was a swimming waltz with 1932 Olympic swimming champion Eleanor Holm (who, for a stormy interval, would be Rose's wife).

The gaudy Aquacades were a far cry from the dignified splendor of the Olympic Games, but Weissmuller didn't care. He had a good time, and the pay added to the tidy income he had begun to make in 1930, when MGM hired him for the role that would transform him into the hero of generations of children at Saturday movie matinees: Tarzan the Ape Man.

Tarzan—the gentle wild man of the jungle invented early in the century by Edgar Rice Burroughs—suited Johnny Weissmuller right down to water level. Being Tarzan was well-paid, regular work. His costume, a loincloth, displayed his magnificent physique, and the role entailed much swimming and lots of physical stunts, which he performed himself. Moreover, there were entertaining costars: Cheetah the chimpanzee, Jackee the lion, and various beautiful actresses. Also, the work wasn't intellectually taxing. Weissmuller himself said he was the only actor in Hollywood who never read a script: His character's vocabulary consisted mostly of "Umgawa," "Me Tarzan, you Jane," "Tarzan hungry, go home, eat," "White man with guns, no good," and, of course, "Tarzan swim now." The plots for the films, which included *Tarzan and the Amazons, Tarzan and the Huntress, Tarzan and the Leopard Women,* and (his 19th and final film, made in 1947) *Tarzan and the Mermaids,* weren't too complicated, either.

In the end, of course, an aging Tarzan proved no more marketable than an aging swimmer: Weissmuller eventually became too middle-aged and portly to play the young hero. But he slid into good fortune once again, switching without complaint to the role of Jungle Jim, a kind of elderly Tarzan in khakis.

Weissmuller's private life was less successful. He drank too much, and his problems with his first four wives—especially the second, the tiny Mexican actress Lupe Velez, known to the press as "Whoopee Lupe"—produced headlines and alimony suits. Extravagant and carefree, he paid little attention to the way his money was managed, and when the job offers faded, in the 1950s, he was left a relatively poor man.

But Weissmuller remained the same: irresponsible, unpretentious, and, like the other swimmers on the 1924 team, sunny natured. Toward the end of his life he suffered a series of crippling strokes that seemed to leave him, at times, a bit unhinged. He spent two years, from 1977 to 1979, in a Los Angeles retirement home for actors, where he was not the most welcome tenant: He had the disconcerting habit of awakening his fellow retirees many mornings with renderings of his famous Tarzan yell. After leaving the home he moved to Acapulco, where he died in 1984. His sunset years had not been without satisfactions; he was, for instance, happily married at last. He told a reporter during those days, "Sure, I've had my problems. Some bad investments. Four marriages that didn't last. Some battles with booze. But I'm a pretty tough guy to sink. I lived an exciting life and I've been an awfully lucky fellow."

The luck that carried Johnny Weissmuller so far had three main components: genetic gifts, native charm—and that first fateful meeting with Bill Bachrach. Indeed, Bachrach's tutelage and Weissmuller's swimming success illustrated the proposition that great coaches and their programs shaped great athletes. Weissmuller's 40 male teammates came from certain universities—notably Stanford and Northwestern—and from men's clubs: five from the Illinois Athletic Club alone. It was the same in many other nations. Boy Charlton and his countryman Richmond Eve (who won the plain high dive in Paris) both learned their skills at the

TARZAN AND THE OLYMPIANS

Hollywood and the Olympic Games both celebrate youth and beauty, so it's little wonder that producers have tapped five former Olympic champions to star as one of the movies' most enduring heroes: Tarzan. The legendary jungle king was created by Edgar Rice Burroughs in 1912 for a comic book story called "Tarzan of the Apes." It told of an English lord, orphaned in infancy and reared by apes in Africa. The tale caught the eye of filmmakers, who first adapted it for the screen in 1918. The original Tarzan was Elmo Lincoln, a broad-chested athletic type who looked good in a loincloth. The mold was cast. The first Olympian Tarzan was

Frank Merrill, an American gymnast from the Antwerp 1920 Games. Merrill starred in *Tarzan the Tiger*, a 1928 release that straddled the silent and sound eras. Unfortunately, his voice wasn't as muscular as his body—a liability even with Tarzan's sparse dialogue. Enter Johnny Weissmuller, who looked and sounded great and was at home in a loincloth. (BVD used him for swimwear ads.) MGM cast Weissmuller in its 1932 remake of *Tarzan the Apeman*, and both audiences and critics loved it. But success breeds competition, and more than one producer had access to the Tarzan property. In 1933, Buster Crabbe, a gold-medal

Tarzan Johnny Weissmuller and his pachyderm pals.

swimmer from the previous year's Olympics in Los Angeles, appeared in an independent feature called *Tarzan the Fearless*. The picture bombed, though Crabbe would soon find fame as sci-fi swashbuckler Flash Gordon. In 1935, Burroughs himself cast Herman Brix, a shot put silver medalist at Amsterdam 1928, in the title role in the *New Adventures of Tarzan*. The film was true to the book, with Brix playing Tarzan as the proper-speaking Lord Greystoke, but it was another box office dud. Weissmuller returned in *Tarzan Escapes*, but cost overruns and three changes of directors made the 1936 release a disaster. Producers blamed the star, and the following year Weissmuller was passed over for *Tarzan's Revenge* in favor of Glenn

Morris, the decathlon champion from Berlin 1936. Eleanor Holm, a swimming gold medalist from Los Angeles 1932, played Jane, his true love. Both actors were long on looks but short on talent, and *Tarzan's Revenge* was a flop. Morris never made another movie. Producers returned to Weissmuller in 1939's *Tarzan Finds a Son*, and the best-loved apeman of them all would reign unchallenged for eight more films. He finally retired from the role in 1948 when contract disputes made him hang up his loincloth for good.

Tarzan Glenn
Morris and his
feline friend
(above).

Tarzan Buster
Crabbe and his
simian sidekick
(right).

Swimmers who competed in Paris were supportive as well as competitive. When they weren't racing, athletes cheered outstanding performances by others. Above, Hawaiian members of the men's team and their friends show their enthusiasm for the women's 100-meter freestylers.

Young American swimmers *(opposite page)* dominated the women's 100-meter freestyle. Ethel Lackie led a 1-2-3 U.S. sweep.

Manly Baths, a swimming club on Sydney harbor. The club was run by the Cavill family, famed swimmers who had taught modern techniques to most Australian athletes. The Swedes trained at the Swedish Swimming Society, a renowned five-pool complex in Stockholm.

For the 18 women on the American team, the situation was much the same, although their opportunities were more limited. By 1924, thanks to a few visionaries, women's athletics had come a long way, developing as men's had, but more slowly. Sports programs appeared at the grander girls' schools and colleges in England and then spread, first to Germany and France (there were women's gymnastics clubs in Germany as early as the 1840s) and then across the sea to America and Australia. But women's programs were quite different from the men's, in some cases because of women's own conflicting fears and hopes and in others because of male pressure. The stern training regimens followed by men were discouraged for women: Prevailing theory held that

too much training would lead to ugly, bulging muscles and perhaps even to sterility. Competition was viewed with suspicion, too: It might make women masculine and coarse, and it exposed them to audiences whose motives for watching might be dubious.

So the women who competed at Paris 1924 were there only on sufferance and only in sports considered appropriate: tennis, fencing, and swimming. The women athletes tended to be defensive, perhaps because they had to cope with an often-hostile press. Influential American sportswriter Paul Gallico, for instance, was a venomous critic. He claimed that the "muscle molls," as he liked to call them, were interested in sports only because they were too homely to attract men, and he wrote that women were incapable of good sportsmanship because they were conditioned to compete viciously among themselves for masculine favor.

No doubt because they were "graceful," Gallico was generally kinder about women swimmers.

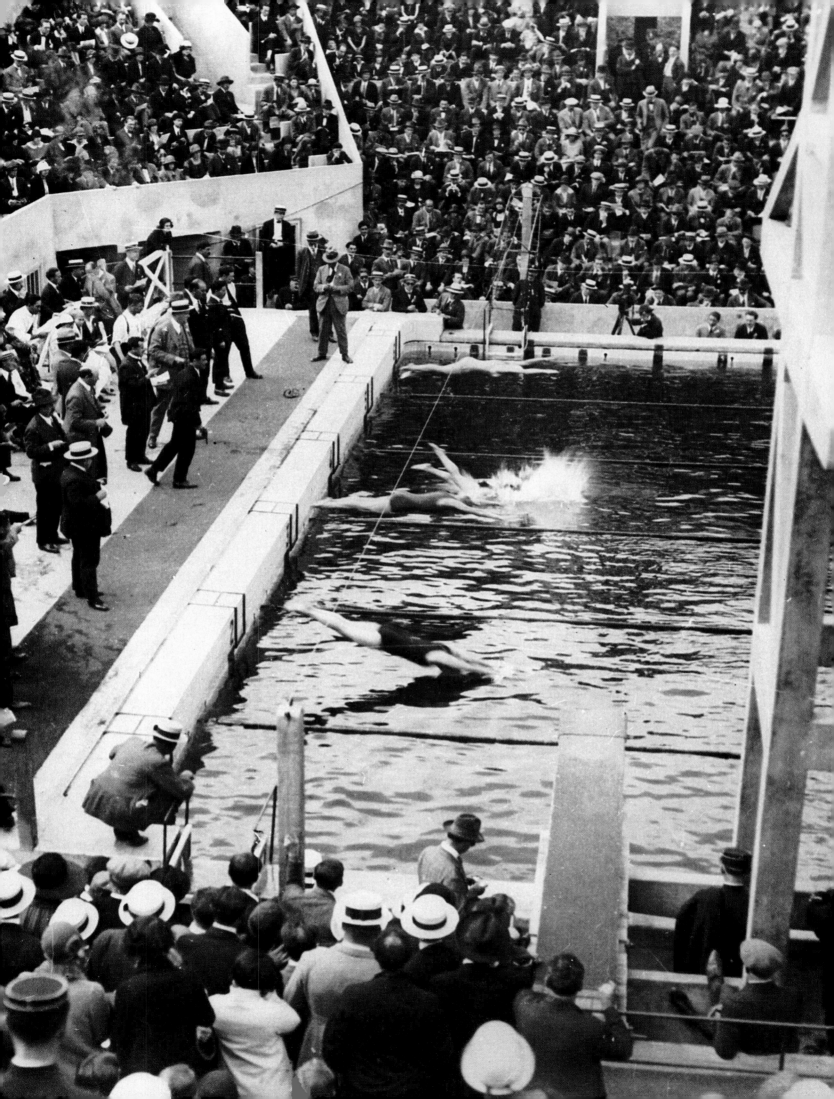

America's Al White finishes the first of four plunges during the platform diving finals. U.S. men would claim all the diving medals except for those in the plain high dive, the specialty that was discontinued after the Paris Games. White won both the platform and springboard events.

He even admired the organization that nurtured them. This was the New York Women's Swimming Association, founded in 1917 by Charlotte Epstein. A career woman and an enthusiastic athlete herself, the redoubtable Mrs. Epstein had persuaded the AAU to register women's swimming and sponsor competition as early as 1914. The WSA wasn't rich; it had only a small pool on the Lower East Side of Manhattan. Divers had to train (at high tide) in a tidal pool at Manhattan

Sybil Bauer practices the backstroke in a tank on board the SS *America* during the American team's passage to France. To keep their athletes fit despite the cramped shipboard facilities, swimming coaches ingeniously wrapped rope around them and made them paddle in place.

Beach, wearing several sweatshirts to protect themselves from injury when they made mistakes. But Charlotte Epstein's athletes were a close-knit, eager group, who gave charity exhibitions and taught swimming to children to raise money for the club. And they were superb swimmers: In the 22 years of Epstein's leadership, they set 51 world records and sponsored 30 national championship relay teams. At the Paris Games, eight of the 18 American swimmers were members of the club. Charlotte Epstein was the team's chief chaperone, and their coach was the man who gave up his spare time to train them for free at her club, Louis deBreda Handley.

This "father of women's swimming" was the counterpart of Bill Bachrach, although his style was more restrained. A fine athlete himself, he competed in football, rowing, water polo, yachting, and swimming. At St. Louis 1904 he had won Olympic golds in water polo and in swimming's 4 x 50-yard freestyle relay, an event since discontinued. Handley was a proselytizer who wrote five books and innumerable newspaper articles about swimming. He was also a master coach who taught his swimmers the newest techniques and looked after their welfare with fierce attention.

The result, in 1924, was a cache of medals for the American women: four golds, four silvers, and three bronzes. There would have been

more, Handley thought, had it not been for the housing, eating, and transportation arrangements in France. His report enriched the jeremiad of American complaints about Rocquencourt: night-long noise from "the tooting of motor horns" on a nearby road, bad food, the muscle-jarring two-hour ride to and from Les Tourelles.

Still, Handley's swimmers swept the 100-meter and 400-meter freestyle races. Martha Norelius took gold in the 400; she was the Swedish-born daughter of a professional coach who had trained at the Swedish Swimming Society. Gentle Sybil Bauer of Chicago, at one time the holder of all existing women's backstroke records, set an Olympic record for the 100-meter backstroke. (Sybil Bauer would die three years later of intestinal cancer. Her fiancé, then-sportswriter Ed Sullivan, was beside her at the end. Her pallbearers were six champion swimmers, among them Johnny Weissmuller.) Aileen Riggin, a tiny, 65-pound teenager, won the bronze medal for the backstroke as well as the silver for springboard diving, the only woman ever to win individual medals in both swimming and diving.

The star of the American team, however, won only bronze medals in the 100- and 400-meter races and a gold in the 400-meter freestyle relay. She went off her form completely, according to Handley, because of the daily battering she got

American Gertrude Ederle knifes through the English Channel's choppy waters in 1926. Expected to win as many as three gold medals in Paris, Ederle took only a pair of bronzes and a share of a relay gold. But the historic Channel swim made her an international celebrity.

while traveling to and from Les Tourelles.

Her name was Gertrude Ederle. The daughter of a German-American butcher, she had been born in Brooklyn in 1906. Shy and quiet, she had dropped out of high school and might simply have disappeared, except that she had an older sister who loved swimming and who encouraged her to join Charlotte Epstein's group. There young Gertrude found her métier. Handley took her in hand and, a year later, turned her loose. She was only 14 then, and she made headlines by beating 51 women in a 3 1/2-mile race across New York Bay. That same year, Ederle broke seven world records—it was the practice then to time swimmers for records at multiple distances throughout a long race—at a 500-meter contest at Brooklyn's Brighton Beach.

Ederle was stoical about her performance in Paris, making no excuse for her poor showing. But when the chance came to swim the English Channel, she jumped at it. No woman had ever swum the bitterly cold currents of this stretch of water—whose width ranges from 21 to 150 miles—although two had tried. Five men had made it, the fastest an Argentinian whose time from the French to the English shore was 16 hours 33 minutes.

Ederle made her first attempt in 1925. It was a failure: Her trainer, fearing she would die of exposure, forced her from the water six and a half miles from the British coast. In 1926, she meant to succeed. (Paul Gallico, although he wrote

about her with uncharacteristic approval, couldn't forbear mean-spirited speculation that the chubby, round-faced girl's lack of beauty inspired her to the effort.)

To get the backing she needed, Ederle had to give up her amateur status. To pay the considerable expenses of transportation, housing, coaches, and companion boats, she signed exclusive story rights over to the *New York News* and the *Chicago Tribune* syndicate, and early in the summer she set up training camp at Cap Gris Nez on the Normandy coast. Her sister Margaret was with her; so were *Chicago Tribune* columnist Westbrook Pegler and his wife and Ederle's coach, Thomas Burgess, who 15 years before had been the second man to swim the Channel. He had made 18 attempts before succeeding.

Gertrude Ederle prepared for her second try in the early hours of August 6. She wore a silk swimming suit and goggles made of a single piece of curved yellow glass. For protection from cold and salt, she was greased from head to toe—first with olive oil, then with lanolin, and then with a horrible mixture of Vaseline and lard. She set off at 7:09 a.m., escorted by a French tugboat and a second small boat carrying, among others, her sister Margaret and her coach.

The sea was fairly calm and the forecast favorable; nevertheless, the swim soon turned into a nightmare. There were unexpected squalls. The sea set up a swift current with battering waves. It was so cold that Burgess and Margaret

Ederle, who joined her sister from time to time for support, could stay in the water no more than a few minutes. At twilight, Burgess, fearing that Gertrude would die of hypothermia or exhaustion, screamed at her, "Trudy, you must come out." Her reply, according to legend, was "What for?" And within the hour, below fading white cliffs, she could see dozens of bonfires twinkling along Dover Beach, lighted by the British to guide her in and welcome her. She staggered into the shore shallows at 9:54 p.m. She had swum 35 miles in 14 hours 31 minutes. The time was two hours and two minutes shorter than that of the fastest man.

Paul Gallico wrote that Ederle's swim was "the greatest recorded athletic feat by a woman in the history of the world." It may have been, but misfortune followed in its wake. Not realizing that she was expected to profit from her venture, Ederle took a three-week trip to Germany's Black Forest to visit her grandmother. During her absence, the man who was handling her finances refused to sign the newspaper or promotion contracts that would have given the now-professional swimmer an income. He was holding out for more money, not suspecting that Ederle's feat would be duplicated by another American woman, Mille Gade Corson, who swam the Channel two weeks after Ederle. Corson took an hour longer, but she was the mother of two children, and this made better copy.

When Ederle finally returned to New York, she got a heroine's welcome. The city gave her a red Buick roadster, her not very grandiose heart's desire. But her amateur status was gone, and, innocent that she was, she'd trusted an agent who lost all her lucrative professional offers. Worse, her hearing was damaged by the swim—by 1933 she was profoundly deaf—and during the thirties she injured her back in an accident that left her in a cast for four years. The result was a nervous breakdown.

Children hung posters along the streets of New York paying tribute to Gertrude Ederle and her Channel swim. Crowds estimated at two million filled the sidewalks of Manhattan to salute the Brooklyn native with a ticker-tape parade.

Ugo Frigerio of Italy throws his arms skyward as he crosses the finish line in the 10,000-meter walk race. Biased judging threatened to turn the walk into a farce, but Frigerio survived protests to defend his title from Antwerp 1920.

She recovered, though, and by all accounts made a success of her diminished life. She earned her living toward the end of the 1930s—along with other women Olympians from 1924, including Martha Norelius and Aileen Riggin—in Billy Rose's Aquacades. She designed clothes. She taught deaf children to swim. During World War II she had a job repairing aircraft parts. In her final interview—given on the 50th anniversary of her Channel swim—she said with her usual sweetness,

"If God called me tomorrow, I'd go willingly. I've had a full life, a beautiful life."

Ederle's remark was typical of the grace of those swimmers of 1924. No matter what direction their lives took, they recalled the Games with the same delight that marked their competition. In fact, the aquatic events were remarkably peaceful: Only one untoward incident occurred, in women's platform

American, one for another—prevented an embarrassing impasse.

Officiating at the Games has always been fraught with controversy, more so in sports like diving, which require subjective assessments, than in track and field, where winning depends on measuring time and distance. Paris in 1924, simmering with nationalistic memories and tensions, had a bountiful share of judging controversies. The 10,000-meter walk race was a farcical example.

Racewalking is a demanding sport, but even walkers concede that it has its comic side. The rules specify that the walker keep one foot on the ground at all times and straighten his lead leg at each step. This engenders an unfortunate waddling effect. It also makes the sport difficult to referee: Judges must watch closely to prevent running, in which both feet leave the ground at once. Walkers are given two cautions for "lifting" (having both feet off the ground); a third lift disqualifies them. Lifting is all too frequent in long races, such as the 10,000 meters, and it has always led to arguments.

It did in Paris, when a large field of racewalkers—so many sweating ducks—took to the street course near Colombes for qualifying heats. They were escorted by a flock of frock-coated judges with their noses to the ground, watching feet. An Austrian named Rudolf Kuhnet was cautioned and then disqualified by an American judge, whom Kuhnet ignored. (He explained afterward that he didn't understand English.) Later in the race, an Italian judge also disqualified him, but since the man spoke in French, Kuhnet ignored him, too. The walker qualified in that heat, and the judges, by now thoroughly incensed, immediately disqualified him—no doubt in German, to make sure he understood. Kuhnet appealed and was reinstated, so outraging the judges that they threatened to quit the Games. This circus continued until the final—postponed for two days because of the quarreling—when all the

diving, and that involved not the contestants, but the judges. Three American divers as well as a Briton, a Dane, and a Swede competed in the finals. Verdicts fell all too obviously along nationalistic lines: The Danish judge voted for the Danish diver, the Swede for the Swedish, and, outdoing them both, the American voted a three-way tie for first among his compatriots. Fortunately, the British and French judges were more level-headed. Their votes—one for one

Two combatants in the team épée competition, Argentine Roberto Larraz *(left)* and Belgian Charles Delporte, duel. Delporte would win the individual épée and lead Belgium to a silver medal in the team event.

problems were solved by Ugo Frigerio, an Italian who won with consummate ease, finishing at least a lap ahead of all but one of his rivals.

Frigerio's victory provided a good day for Italy—and those weren't all that frequent. A beautiful land with a glorious past, Italy was nevertheless the poor relation of Europe, and Italians were all too aware of it. For centuries their nation had been on the decline, constantly conquered, always fragmented. Even the unification of the various Italian states in the mid-19th century created no more than an impoverished country with a weak, discredited government open to domination by anyone who wanted it. Italy had entered World War I on the side of the Allies, but it entered late, and its poor performance made it more a burden than a help. After the war, the villainous Benito Mussolini and his Fascists swept into power in the elections held in the spring of 1924—

elections that had almost certainly been fixed. Mussolini's chief critic was murdered and mutilated, at his orders, as he later boasted. All of Europe knew about it.

So Italian competitors at Paris 1924 had a long history of reasons to be defensive, and their various tensions helped inspire the posturing that marred the fencing competitions.

Fencing, with its aristocratic origins, archaic French terminology, and elegant white accoutrements, is a sport that lends itself to drama. Competition with any of its three weapons—the light foil, slightly heavier épée, and saber—requires intelligence, concentration, and feline speed and precision, and tournaments often are highly charged. In addition, wins are decided by the number of times a fencer hits his rival, and before the days of electronic devices that register them, determining hits fairly wasn't easy. It entailed an extensive cast of characters: Each match—fought on a 2 x 14-meter course known as a *piste*—required four judges and a president to oversee their work. And fencing tournaments are lengthy and tiring: Individual medals are awarded after a series of rounds and a final elimination showdown. In team fencing, every member of each team fights every member of its opposition.

The 1924 tournament was held in the old Vélodrome d'Hiver, a glass-roofed cycling arena not far from the Eiffel Tower, an arena where Ernest Hemingway sometimes watched people race on wooden tracks in the smoky light of Paris afternoons. Now the skylight magnified the summer heat, and athletes and spectators sweated. The audience was large, partisan, and knowledgeable, comprehending the language of *prime*, *sixte*, and *quarte*, of *balestra* and *flèche*, of *riposte* and *remise*. These aficionados had come to see the Italians and the French, long famous rivals; and the Hungarians, the finest saber fencers in the world.

By the time the team foil tournament reached its final pools, emotions were running high. The finalists were the French and the Italians, and whoever won would go on to win the gold medal. By the fifth match the French were in the lead, with their champion, the incomparable Lucien Gaudin, pitted against Italian Aldo Boni. The men were tied at four touches each before a hushed crowd, when—following a swift and complex interchange—the judges awarded the winning point to Gaudin. Losing his temper completely, Boni launched a stream of abuse at a Hungarian judge named Kovacs. The judge immediately sought out the Jury of Appeal, a five-member panel that adjudicated disputes, to demand an apology. Boni's reaction was to deny that he had said anything, but Kovacs had a witness, an Italian who coached the Hungarian team. His name was Italo Santelli. When, without much enthusiasm, Santelli confirmed the judge's accusation, the Italian foil team stomped out, singing Fascist hymns and

loudly cheered by their countrymen. The Italians thereby forfeited the match.

There would be repercussions later, but Kovacs—who seems to have had an unpleasant Games, all in all—and the Italians were not finished with each other. Several days later, after the Italians had defeated the Hungarians in the team saber competition, the fencers met again for individual sabers. Four Italians and three Hungarians qualified for the finals, and the Italians were requested to fight off against each other. Their leader, Oreste Puliti, beat the other three with ease, to no one's surprise. But the judges, led by Kovacs, accused the Italians of throwing their fights to give Puliti the best chance at the gold.

Puliti's response was to threaten the judge with a caning. He was disqualified, and—again—all the Italians walked out. Sandor Posta of Hungary eventually won the saber competition.

A few days later, the affair descended further into farce. Oreste Puliti, obviously still seething and out for vengeance, ran into Kovacs in a music hall and began shouting at him. Kovacs replied that he didn't speak Italian and so couldn't understand the argument. In proper theatrical fashion, Puliti then hit Kovacs in the face and said perhaps he would understand *that*. To prevent a fight there and then, Puliti's companions proposed a formal duel.

That this mode of settling arguments could be seriously proposed in 1924 tells some-

A participant's badge from the 1924 Games.

The fashionable gather for the Olympic polo competition at the St. Cloud Country Club in suburban Paris.

thing about how different the world was then. Although dueling had been illegal in Great Britain for almost 40 years, it had been outlawed in France only recently. In Germany it had been outlawed after World War I, but the Nazis would revive it in the 1930s, and it would continue through the short duration of the Third Reich. The Italians, who didn't believe their laws could protect private honor, had elevated dueling to an art form. Their bible, still in use in the 1960s, was the *Codice cavalleresco italiano*— the *Italian Code of Chivalry*. First published in 1887 (and reprinted 18 times), it had been written by a cavalry colonel named Jacopo Gelli, who provided his readers with exhaustive information, including model letters and details about dress, procedure, and participants.

No doubt Puliti put the book to use. In any case, he and Kovacs, with their seconds, met four months later near a town at the border between Hungary and Yugoslavia. Their duel lasted a correct and bloody hour, after which they were separated and, honor being satisfied,

shook hands. Puliti was disqualified for life from competing in the Olympic Games.

Even this was not the last of the quarrels. Well after the Games had ended, the Italian foils team took it upon itself to issue a statement claiming that Italo Santelli had supported Kovacs because he thought that otherwise his Hungarians would lose to them. Santelli promptly challenged the Italian team captain to his own duel. The fencing master was over 60, and guided, perhaps, by Colonel Gelli's little book, his son demanded that he be allowed to replace the older man. The combatants eventually met for a heavy saber duel, which was halted as soon as Santelli the younger slashed open the Italian fencer's head. No one died. Santelli the younger went on to a long career as a teacher of the sport.

Dueling aside, fencers are rarely injured in competition: The contestants are protected by masks, pads, and gloves, and by blunting devices for their weapons. In any case, fencing is play: The goal is to touch

Nº 1005.- OLYMPIC GAMES 1924
Polo Contest - Spain against U.S.A.

America's Fred Roe edges past a Spanish rival to attempt a shot in the Olympic polo tournament. The United States beat Spain 15-2 on its way to the finals against Argentina. The Argentines won the tournament 6-5 on a last-second goal.

America's eight-oared shell and its Yale crew come to rest after victory. The Yale eight used a novel rowing technique developed by its coach, Ed Leader. The new style needed taller athletes such as 6-foot-4 Benjamin Spock *(third from right)* to compensate for the shortened stroke. Long after his Olympic glory, Spock would earn greater fame as a pediatrician, an author, and a political activist.

your opponent, not to hurt him. In boxing, on the other hand, harm is the whole point. The sport has its safeguards, but the boxer's goal is to damage the other man. The entire exercise is one of violence and aggression, and these, like any strong emotions, are infectious in a crowd. Boxing crowds tend to be nasty.

Furthermore, boxing is difficult to judge. Theoretically, points are awarded in each round (three in Olympic matches) for hits, blocks, knockdowns, and so on; in truth, choosing winners (except when there is a knockout) is highly subjective. It's impossible for referees and judges to see every action in a fast-moving bout. The winner of any given boxing round is the man officials believe scored the most.

Boxing judgments were particularly subjective at Paris because—to the disgust of competing teams—the referees stood outside the ring,

where their views were limited. This and the overwrought nationalism of the boxing fans created scenes that made the fencing incidents look wanly genteel.

Some of the passion derived not just from the normal moods of boxing crowds, but from the sport's recent history. After its heyday in Classical Rome, it had fallen into decline for centuries. It was revived in 18th-century England and gradually regulated. In 1743 boxers replaced the formless and dangerous ring of spectators with a squared-off area of defined size (which they continued to call a ring) and outlawed such moves as hitting below the belt. This made the sport only slightly less brutal, as appears from the Marquess of Queensberry's boxing rules, which were established in 1866 and govern the modern game. Among other things, the rules limited the number of rounds

American pugilists look suitably tough as they pose for a group picture before leaving for Paris. Fidel La Barba *(front, far left)* and Jackie Fields *(second from left)* would win gold medals.

fought, made gloves mandatory, and outlawed gouging and wrestling. Weight divisions, from light flyweight to super heavyweight, appeared in the decades that followed.

Certainly there were some gentlemen pugilists, most of them in Britain. But, in the main, boxing remained a rough, dirty, backroom contest. The atmosphere at fights wasn't far removed from that at badger baiting or cockfighting, and the bouts were uncomfortable and often dangerous to attend. Fans had to fight for their seats.

In the United States, all this changed in 1921 when a promoter named George L. Rickard (known as Tex, after the state where he had been a gambling dealer before moving up in the world) made boxing respectable. Reasoning that if he could attract women he could sell two tickets for every one, he organized his venues so that ladies would feel safe and comfortable. Rickard's arenas had numbered aisles and reserved seats, and he kept the places orderly with a large and thoroughly trained staff of ushers, firemen, and special police. Besides that, he picked his fighters carefully for skill

and appeal, arranged dramatic confrontations, and advertised them cleverly.

The result was the first professional prizefight to take a million dollars in gate receipts. It was held on July 2, 1921, in Jersey City, New Jersey. The contestants were heavyweights: Georges Carpentier, the champion of France, and the American Jack Dempsey. From an international point of view, Carpentier was the hero. He was a brave veteran of the Great War; he was blonde, handsome and debonair; he could dance well and sing the songs of the French boulevards. Jack Dempsey was the villain. Dark and beetle-browed, he was an inarticulate, truculent man and a savage fighter. He was also appreciably bigger than Carpentier, and he won the fight by a knockout. It was for this famous defeat that Parisians wept in the streets. The memory of it didn't improve the mood at the Vélodrome d'Hiver, where the Olympic boxing matches were staged three years later.

Some very good boxers fought in Paris. Among the American team were four fighters trained at the Los Angeles Athletic Club by its coach,

Chief Warrant Officer Morris Fisher readies his weapon during the free rifle competition. The U.S. Marine finished first in the individual and team event. In two Games, Antwerp 1920 and Paris 1924, Fisher would win five gold medals, the record for most Olympic shooting championships for an American.

George Blake. Blake's program was one of those—like Bill Bachrach's at the Illinois Athletic Club or Louis deBreda Handley's in New York—that consistently discovered and nurtured fine athletes. His boxers were poor teenagers, and he not only trained them but also saw that they were rewarded with groceries.

Of the close-knit four, Ed Allegrini forfeited his chance to box in Paris when he donated his blood to transfuse a teammate who had suffered internal injuries during shipboard practice. Fidel La Barba (who would go on as a professional to win the world championship) took the gold medal in the flyweight class.

And Jackie Fields and Joe Salas—schoolmates, clubmates, and good friends—reached the finals in the featherweight class only to discover that they were to fight each other.

They were just boys: Fields was 16 and Salas 18. They dressed in the same room, and Salas would remember, "When they knocked on the door to call us to the fight, we looked up at each other and started to cry and hugged. Ten minutes later we were beating the hell out of each other." Fields won. He threw his arms around Salas to say he was sorry; then he returned to the dressing room and wept again. Subsequent to the Games there were two rematches. Fields

RIGOULOT RULES

The weight-lifting competition at Paris was a showcase for Frenchman Charles Rigoulot. A neighborhood tough as a teenager, Rigoulot turned to honest work when he landed a job as a printer's apprentice. The ease with which the 16-year-old handled the heavy lithograph stones attracted the attention of Jean Dame, an established weight trainer who was in search of new talent. In three months Dame turned Rigoulot into a national champion, and by 1924 the trainer's protégé was ready for the world's best. So effortless were Rigoulot's lifts at the Games that observers thought the weights were mislabeled.

He outlifted his closest competitor by 27 1/2 pounds (12.5 kilograms) to take the light heavyweight division. Rigoulot continued to improve after the Games, and within a year he earned the title of "World's Strongest Man" during an exhibition in Paris. Age pushed him out of competition in the 1930s, but he continued to star in French sport as a champion race driver for Peugeot. During World War II, Rigoulot became a symbol of resistance when he was jailed for striking a Nazi officer. Set free after France was liberated, the strongman remained a national hero until his death in 1962.

During a 1925 weight-lifting performance in Paris, Charles Rigoulot shows why he was called the strongest man in the world. Rigoulot was light heavyweight champion at Paris 1924. His fast-lifting style changed the carnival-like atmosphere of strength exhibitions into true competitions.

CHARLES RIGOULOT
l'Homme le plus fort du monde

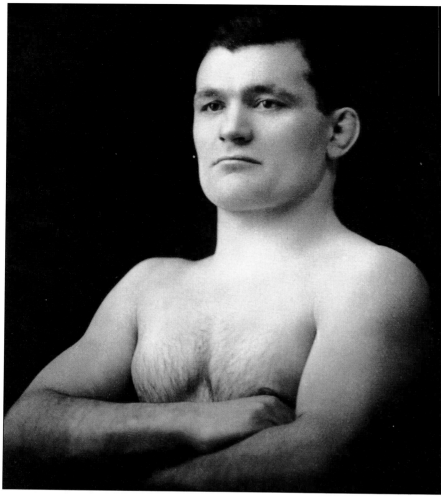

Finnish Greco-Roman wrestler Oskari Friman won a gold medal in Antwerp 1920 as a fly-weight. He moved up to the lightweight division in Paris and came away with another championship. Finland was as impressive in wrestling as it was in distance running. In both mat specialties, Greco-Roman and freestyle, Finns captured 16 of the 39 medals in contention.

won both. Salas never spoke to him again.

In sum, American boxers won two gold medals, two silver, and two bronze at Paris 1924. They might have won more, they thought, if it hadn't been for incompetent referees and judges.

For the Americans, the most irritating judgment of all came in the bantamweight semifinals, when Joe Lazarus of Cornell University fought Oscar Andren of Sweden. Lazarus, according to the entertaining report of his coach, was clearly winning when, toward the end of the match, he "let loose with a right-hand hook, which found a resting place plumb on Andren's chin, which knocked him to the canvas as dead as a doornail." Coach Blake was speaking figuratively. Andren survived the clean knockout. The referee then disqualified Lazarus for what he said was hitting during a clinch. The Americans were furious and the Swedes so mortified that they offered a re-match. Olympic officials wouldn't allow it.

The audiences staged a number of hostile demonstrations against America, the coaches

noted. In truth, the audience staged hostile demonstrations at every opportunity, and against sundry targets. During early welterweight bouts, the British referee, T. H. Walker, disqualified an Italian boxer for repeated holding. The man fell to the canvas in floods of tears, and the Italian fans went wild. Screaming invective, they rained sticks, coins, and other paraphernalia onto the referee, who eventually was escorted to safety by a guard of heavyweights.

The scene was a fitting preliminary to the welterweight finals, fought between Jean Delarge of Belgium and Hector Mendez of Argentina. Mendez was behind on points in the first two rounds, but in the third, he pummeled the Belgian all over the ring. This was a spectacular conclusion to the fight, but Delarge's lead was such that he won the verdict. That announcement brought hundreds of Argentinians screaming to their feet for their hero and booing the Belgian anthem. One of Delarge's supporters waded into the crowd waving a Belgian flag, and fights broke out in the stands. It took 15 minutes to calm the fans down. Hardly had they begun to settle, though, when a matchless combination of suspect judging and national fervor produced one of the most bizarre incidents of the Games.

This episode came in the middleweight finals, when the British champion, Jack Mallin (who had never been beaten) met Roger Brousse, a Frenchman and naturally a great favorite. Mallin appeared to lead handily throughout. At the end of the three rounds, he complained to the referee—who ignored him—that Brousse had bitten his chest. It was true: There were clear tooth marks. The British chose not to register a formal complaint, but when the judges awarded the fight to Brousse, Swedish officials called in the Jury of Appeal. This group, meeting late into the night, heard and saw evidence that included Brousse's tooth marks on some of his earlier opponents. Faced with this information, the French claimed the bites were uninten-

Souvenir des Jeux Olympiques

PARIS 1924

DIX

tional. Brousse inadvertently snapped his teeth when he threw a punch, they said, and sometimes opponents' chests got in the way. Unable to reach agreement, the jury retired, to meet again the following night. In the end, in what must be a compromise of unparalleled unwisdom, they accepted Brousse's curious explanation. Then they disqualified him.

They chose to announce this decision on the night of the boxing finals, during the pandemonium following the Mendez-Delarge fight. Brousse, at ringside, burst into sobs. (Weeping seems to have been endemic at these matches.) French fans, adding their own screams to those of the Argentinians and Belgians, carried their hero shoulder high around the Vélodrome, started their own fights, and charged the ring, where Mallin was trying to fight his final against John Elliott, another Briton. Nobody could see enough of the fight to describe it, but it was said to be close and—unsurprisingly, considering the circumstances—uninspired. Mallin won.

The boxing turmoil prompted the *Times* of London to apocalyptically prophesy the end of Olympism. In a July 22 article headed "Olympic Games Doomed/Failure of the Ideal/Disgraceful Scenes," the *Times* said that Paris 1924 had "demonstrated with dreadful clearness that the Games exacerbate international bitternesses instead of soothing them." An article the following day accused the French of mismanaging the Games. Reacting predictably, the French press called the *Times* "the enemy of France." There was a flurry of correspondence on the always-lively *Times* letters page, plus a spate of articles querying whether Britain should continue to participate in the Games.

It was a tempest in a press teacup and it was over in a few days. Still, the matter received more attention perhaps than even the special correspondent had hoped. Most of this attention was negative. But veteran journalist H. Perry Robinson, writing in a periodical called *The Nineteenth Century and After*, showed a thoughtful awareness of just how much sport, and the world, were changing. Robinson pointed out

Winning cyclists and gymnasts adorn a keepsake from the Paris Games. Souvenir dealers had already established a foothold at the Olympic Games, offering postcards and pins for anyone who wanted a memento of the sports festival.

Vincent Richards was among the Americans who swept all five tennis titles in Paris. Richards won the men's singles and with his partner, Frank Hunter, the Olympic men's doubles championship.

that some of Britain's reputation for greatness had rested on her athletic prowess, now in decline: "It was our example which inspired the peoples of the world to make themselves into athletes; and having started, they have bettered our methods until with each decade, with each Olympiad, we become less and less the leading nation, and our reputation falls lower and lower from its former high estate."

Robinson said that if Britain withdrew from the Games, the world would say the nation could not take a beating, that it was "the worst of all kinds of sportsman, the kind that sulks in defeat and will not play again." And while acknowledging Britain's sentimental love of amateurism, of the village green and the school playing field, Robinson wrote that training—in America, in Finland—had produced sterling performances in Paris. Britain needed to overcome her prejudices and train her youth in athletics, he wrote, in the interests of a fit nation: "It is not a question, as is often sneeringly suggested, of 'breeding champions'; but for every champion that is bred we breed 500 near-champions, and fire by his example the emulation of 5,000 more."

The old ways were passing. Sport was moving into an age of expertise and specialization.

All the factors that were affecting sport in that Golden Age—international competition; the press; the questions of training, of money, and of women athletes—were dramatically displayed in international tennis. Most particularly, they were manifest in the rivalry between Suzanne Lenglen of France and Helen Wills of the United States. It was only one stage in the cycle of the rise and fall of tennis champions, but it attracted attention because of the matchless talent of the two women and the dramatic contrasts between them.

The game they played was evolving during those years. It descended from the indoor sport known in Britain as real tennis, in the U.S. as court tennis, and in France as *jeu de paume* (because it was first played with the palms of the hands). This was a sport of princes: The few remaining European structures for the original game include that of Henry VIII at Hampton Court Palace outside London, which is still in use. Adapted for the stately lawns of England by Major Walter Clopton Wingfield, tennis became the perfect sport for carefully chaperoned young men and women of privilege. It was one of the few games they could play together freely, and it swiftly spread to the Continent, the U.S., and Australia. Before long, it was organized in the manner of other sports: The tournaments at Wimbledon, which were tantamount to world championships, were established in 1871; the U.S. championships in 1881; the French in 1891; and the Australian in 1905. The Davis Cup, the great reward for international supremacy, was first contested in 1900.

Women's tennis was initially quite a different game from men's. Constricted by corsets, petticoats, stockings, and long white dresses, women played a slow, gentle game. They served underhand and competed with high lobs (called "moonballs") from the baseline. Skill was defined by placement of the ball.

The genteel game began to change as society—and women's sports—developed in the early years of the 20th century. Suzanne Lenglen would be the pioneer. By the time she was born in 1899, France had a well-established tennis circuit, profitable for private tennis clubs and often for the athletes as well. The season began in winter, with club tournaments on the Riviera—which until the later 1920s was a winter, not a summer, resort for the rich—and moved north to St. Cloud outside Paris for the spring World Hard Court Championships. All this play led to the World Championships at Wimbledon in June.

Suzanne Lenglen grew up in the right place to learn the game. Her father, living comfortably on inherited income, had a vacation villa in Nice.

Charles and Anaïs Lenglen flank daughter Suzanne during a break in a tennis match. Charles is remembered as the first in a long line of terrible tennis fathers.

He was fascinated by tennis strategy and tactics and impressed by the lavish treatment the stars enjoyed. He gave his daughter a racquet when she was 11—a mixed blessing: Her obvious athletic facility transformed Lenglen into one of those monster tennis fathers who crop up in the game from time to time.

Observing and then using the best techniques of men's play, Lenglen schooled Suzanne mercilessly, day after day. Hour after hour she practiced a single stroke from one position on the court. When she had mastered it, he taught her placement and control, using first handkerchiefs laid on the court, then coins. Eventually she could return any shot to any target he specified, and she could do it hundreds of times in succession. Besides all this, the father saw to it that his daughter pursued a rigorous regimen of swimming and running. He kept her at it, and kept her winning, with manipulative swings between affection and praise when she did well and abusive ridicule when she didn't. He was always loudly at courtside when Suzanne played.

Lenglen's paternal tyranny produced an eccentric and pitiably neurotic woman, completely dependent on the man who'd shaped her. Her only refuge from her dreadful routine was illness, real or invented. But her tennis was incomparable. It had the transparency of art: It seemed unstudied and effortless. The French tennis star René Lacoste, who had expected extraordinary strokes from Suzanne, was disappointed when first he observed the uncomplicated nature of her game; he said she played the simplest strokes in the world. Then he added, "It was only after several games that I understood what harmony was concealed by her simplicity, what wonderful mental and physical balance was hidden by the facility of her play." Her opponents, including Helen Wills, had the same reactions: She made the game look so easy that it was only when you faced her from the other side of the net that you realized how good she was, how flawless her control, how uncanny her anticipation of any move her opponent might make. Others compared her to a chess master

who dominates the board from the first move and forces competitors to play her game.

By 1919, when, having swept through the French championships, she won the first of her six Wimbledon titles, Lenglen was a media goddess and a French national treasure. Sportswriters were inspired to ecstatic flights: She was, they wrote, "like the movement of fire over prairie grass. She serves with all the male athlete's power. She smashes with the same loose and rapid action. Her volley is not a timid push but an arrow from the bow." Graceful as a dancer, always in movement, she was likened to a butterfly and to the huntress goddess Diana.

After 1919, Lenglen played up to the developing legend. A big-boned, hawk-nosed woman

Suzanne Lenglen, 15, practices on her home court, the Riviera's Nice Tennis Club, in 1915. Lenglen's father saw to it that she devoted all her time to exacting drills. His tyranny made her unbeatable— and flamboyantly unstable.

with bad, protruding teeth, she acquired in movement something approaching beauty. Thus her clothes emphasized movement. She dispensed with corsets and heavy cotton; instead, she wore costumes made for her by the couturier of sport, Jean Patou—translucent, fluttering silk skirts cut just to the knee, sleeveless silk blouses, a bandeau for her hair of twisted silk held in place by a diamond brooch, light sweaters in pastels that matched the bandeau. She wore makeup on court—shocking to many, then—and a gold bracelet above her left elbow.

The French adored it: Lenglen could do no wrong. She won the women's singles gold medal at Antwerp 1920 (where she referred to herself without embarrassment or irony as "the great Lenglen"), and from that time she was described in France as *hors classe*: Other players might be ranked, but Lenglen was beyond classification.

Lenglen's skill made her a golden goose to the Nice Tennis Club. Anytime she appeared, she drew enormous crowds, not to mention tourists who spent money in the resort's casinos, restaurants, and hotels. All sorts of financial arrangements were made with her father. *Bons*—orders at stores for 1,000 francs, which could be traded for cash and which all champions got—were only the beginning. The Nice Tennis Club paid her family's expenses for travel, hotels, and food, and they financed the Lenglen house. She always played at that club.

Players of other nations were sometimes sour about her, although everyone acknowledged the splendor of her play. The U.S. men's champion, Bill Tilden, thought she looked like a cross between a prima donna and a streetwalker. He made it a point to tempt her into playing an exhibition with him so that he could beat her, simply to show that the best women were no match for the best men—a sign, perhaps, of what a threat she seemed to him. And he was openly hostile when she appeared in America.

Lenglen had to appear in America. She was claiming the title of world champion, but the U.S. Lawn Tennis Association (USLTA) didn't acknowledge that Wimbledon winners were world champions. Journalists were pressing for a match for the U.S. title between Lenglen and the Norwegian-born Molla Mallory. Known as "Iron Molla," Mallory had held the U.S. championship six times since 1915. Lenglen had, in fact, beaten her—but only just—at St. Cloud.

So Suzanne Lenglen traveled to America in a fanfare of publicity in 1921 to play Mallory at Forest Hills. East Coast tennis clubs vied to get her for exhibitions. The USLTA agreed, despite Prohibition, to let her have the iced and sugared cognac she required during games.

Such concessions notwithstanding, the American trip was a disaster. Other players at Forest Hills—notably Tilden—gave their exotic visitor a chilly welcome, and so did the audience. The effect on this high-strung personality was obvious: Lenglen's game fell apart, and at the end of her first set, with Mallory clearly winning, the Frenchwoman walked to the umpire's chair and claimed she was too faint to continue. Convention demanded that no one cheat an opponent of a victory by this kind of default unless he actually had to be carried off the court. There was low but audible hissing from the stands. And there was loud hissing from the American press when reporters discovered that the supposedly swooning Lenglen had spent the evening dancing.

The reaction in France was indignant. There were angry exchanges between the French Tennis Federation and its American counterpart. Even fervent French defenders, however, could not restore their darling's international claims.

Lenglen did this herself, during the 1922 season, taking title after title on the Riviera, at St. Cloud, and at Wimbledon, where in a bitter and widely reported confrontation, she defeated Molla Mallory. She beat her again when Mallory chased her to the Riviera for a rematch. Mallory, as every top player eventually is, was being pushed from her place. Later that year she lost her American title at Forest Hills, and the cycle of challenge and defeat began again, with new players.

The athlete who took Mallory's title was Helen Wills. Just 18 years old, she had been climbing through the ranks of the sport since her first tournament appearance in 1919.

Wills' advent at this particular time was tonic for international tennis, not only because of her out-size talent, but because she was such a perfect foil for Suzanne Lenglen. The two were as different in family, personality, appearance, and style as Jack Dempsey and Georges Carpentier. They provided the kind of classic contrast between New World and Old that early 20th-century novelists and poets—and journalists—loved to explore.

Born in California in 1905, Helen Wills was the beloved only child of a surgeon and a teacher whose sole pupil was her daughter: The mother taught her bright girl at home until the child was eight and entered public school. That same year, Helen's father gave her a tennis racquet and showed her the basics of the game. She liked it.

California was a good place to learn. Tennis, introduced there in the 1880s, was the most popular sport in the state. Because the dry summers made grass difficult to maintain, most courts were asphalt or concrete, and there were thousands of them—in private yards, in tennis clubs, and in the public parks of every city and town. You could play for free in California all year round. Furthermore, women's tennis was taken more seriously there than elsewhere. As early as the 1890s, women practiced against men and played an adaptation of the hard-hitting men's game. By the early decades of the new century, California was beginning to produce national and international champions.

Helen Wills' rise to stardom began after the Great War, when her family moved to Berkeley and she started to play seriously. She realized, she later said, that the imaginative playacting she had loved in childhood wasn't possible as she

grew older: Tennis, she thought, was its counterpart. She wanted to be good at it. Playing on public courts, almost always winning, she attracted the attention of experts.

One of them was the coach of the Berkeley Tennis Club, William C. "Pop" Fuller, who taught her placement, control, and anticipation and tried to introduce finesse to her mighty strokes. Another was Hazel Hotchkiss Wightman, American champion from 1909 through 1911 and again in 1919. Wightman was also a 1924 Olympic champion, winning in mixed doubles and, with Wills, in women's doubles. A fellow Californian, Wightman first saw Helen Wills play in 1920. So impressed was the older woman that for weeks she spent hours every day working with Wills. Both Wightman and Fuller spoke of their pupil with pride. Fuller felt his greatest achievement was working with her. Wightman, who would never lose a match

An official Press badge for the 1924 Games.

Suzanne Lenglen (*left*) and Helen Wills take the court before their 1926 match in Cannes. The pair made as big an impact on fashion as they did on tennis.

SPORT ET COUTURE

The emerging independence of the postwar women in the 1920s created a demand for new fashion. Among couturiers who heeded the call early was Parisian designer Jean Patou. "My clothes are made to practice *le sport*," he explained while showing his collection in 1924. "I have aimed at making them pleasant to the eye and allowing absolute liberty of movement." Liberty was quite a novelty; corset-bound prewar fashions had encumbered any activity more strenuous than a stroll. The sleek Patou silks that freed the female frame quickly found favor with Suzanne Lenglen, who sported one of his sleeveless blouses and calf-length pleated skirts at Wimbledon in 1919. The look created a sensation and became Lenglen's signature, and the rage for sport chic was on. Patou's biggest following was in America, whose women had a reputation in Europe for being active, slender, and tan. Helen Wills soon joined Patou's clientele. With the trend clearly visible, other designers joined the ready-to-wear revolution. By the end of the decade, many labels featured sportswear for the modern woman.

as Wills' doubles partner, remembered the shy child with affection and delighted in the magnificent blossoming of her skill.

The mentors' generosity and loyalty contrasted starkly with Wills' own ungraciousness. When she became a star, she would repeatedly claim that she was a natural champion, self-taught. "I have never had a professional lesson in my life," she told journalists, "nor any help from really good players, either."

The lack of gratitude was one facet of Wills' curious character. A prim, serious child, she grew in the years between 1920 and 1924 into a prim, serious woman. Not for her the flamboyance of a Lenglen: She wore no makeup (nor did she need it; she was simply and classically beautiful), and her costume in the early days was a decorous white pleated skirt with a middy blouse. Unlike the flappers of the period, with whom she was repeatedly (and favorably) compared, she didn't bob her hair. It was left long, worn in braids when she was younger, coiled into buns as she grew up. Her trademark was a white sun visor.

She was formidable. She was big—5 feet 7 inches, 150 pounds—and she was strong. She played a man's game with a service more powerful than any of her rivals', confident volleying from the net, and daunting ground strokes. She played her opponents into exhaustion. One rival said that Wills hit the ball so hard that it seemed to have been dipped in concrete, and you could feel the impact of her shots in your arm and shoulder as you returned them.

And Wills had killer instinct. The graces of the game seemed to elude her. She never smiled at opponents, and she never spoke when changing courts. When asked about this, she said she didn't believe in encouraging the competition: "I want it to be understood that we are in a battle, not a social affair."

Literal-minded, humorless, severely formal, self-absorbed ("I was not curious about people,

nor did I wonder why they behaved as they did"), Wills concentrated implacably on her game. In the early 1920s she began to attract a great deal of attention as she worked her way up the U.S. championship ladder. Journalists' views of her varied. The dean of American sports reporters, Grantland Rice, thought she represented the power but not the romance of youth. Observing her emotionless demeanor, he eventually concluded that it was not a facade but the truth: She had no great emotions—other than the will to win.

Rice noted, however, that Wills never made excuses when she lost. By 1923, he was describing the "peacefulness and perfection" of her strokes. Her game was invincible, he said: "It required a combination of tennis genius and amazing patience and long, hard practice to get this result." (Wills repeatedly stated that she rarely practiced; again, she guarded her self-image as a natural genius.) Paul Gallico—who thought tennis was an upper-class sissy's game in any case—described her as a social-climbing snob. But even he admired her power and determination. As for the rest, they gave her nicknames, chief among them "the American Girl": Wills, to many, represented the best of modern youth—clean living, healthy, athletic, handsome, and well behaved. The opposite, in short, of Suzanne Lenglen.

Journalists began to talk about a Lenglen-Wills confrontation after Wills took the U.S. championship from Molla Mallory in 1923. That autumn Wills entered the University of California to study painting, emphasizing that tennis was just a game to her and claiming that "art will be my life." Nevertheless, no one believed that she would miss the opportunity to play against the best.

The chance came in 1924, the year that Lenglen would seek her sixth straight Wimbledon title. It was also the year of the Olympic Games—and Lenglen was the defending champion.

Suzanne, always fragile, seemed to be pushed near the edge by the prospect of a contest with Wills. In the early spring of 1924, she won the Southern France championship, but her form and coordination were off. She said she had jaundice. In fact, she had gained weight during the winter, and it slowed her. Throughout the spring there were anorexic episodes, hysterical tantrums, and sudden withdrawals from tournaments.

Still, by early summer, a match with Helen Wills seemed inevitable. The American went to England to compete at the Wightman Cup. (Originally a sort of Davis Cup for women, the event was named after Hazel Wightman, who had donated its trophy.) Lenglen crossed the Channel to watch her rival play. Unused to grass courts, Wills played poorly in the Wightman singles, although, with Hazel Wightman, she won the doubles.

Becoming more confident on the new surface as Wimbledon began, Wills won steadily through her matches until the final. There she lost to Kathleen McKane, who thus became the first British woman since 1914 to win the Wimbledon title. The reason Wills played McKane and not Lenglen was that Lenglen was overwrought, out of shape, exhausted by her own early contests, and probably too fearful or too fragile to go on. She withdrew partway through the tournament, claiming jaundice. None of the Americans believed her. Pop Fuller remarked that he didn't know about jaundice, but Lenglen seemed yellow

Helen Wills (left) stands next to France's Didi Vlasto, her opponent in the women's tennis finals at Paris. Wills easily won the singles and, with Hazel Wightman, the women's doubles crown.

to him. Within the week, Lenglen also withdrew from the Olympic Games.

Helen Wills, having just lost to McKane, made no comment on Lenglen's departure. She crossed the Channel with America's Olympic tennis team and settled into a hotel on the Champs Élysées.

It was her first visit to Paris. The city entranced her. She liked the crowds and the noise; she liked watching the farm carts piled with carrots passing along the great boulevard at night; she liked the museums and galleries and shops. The city had an elegance lacking in America.

She was less enchanted with Colombes, approached through a landscape of "factories, rough cobbled streets, small, depressing looking dwellings and dirty corner cafés," as she noted. The tennis stadium was only partly finished when first she saw it. And the arrangements for the tennis players—no running water, no towels, no place to rest—left so much to be desired that Julian Myrick, captain of the U.S. men's team, threatened a boycott. Even when the courts were finished and the facilities improved, there were problems—noise, guns going off at the track, ball boys who refused to fetch balls in the heat, umpires who didn't appear, vendors hawking Eskimo Pies and fruit and ices in the stands.

Still, a number of enthusiastic American fans were on hand, and they had reason to cheer. Their tennis team won every gold medal: men's and women's singles and doubles, mixed doubles. Calm and confident on the red clay courts, Helen Wills became the first American woman to win an important international title since 1907.

She won the Olympic gold medal in women's singles by defeating Didi Vlasto, the reigning French women's champion in Lenglen's absence. The two women played before a raucous crowd. Vlasto arrived late, having forgotten her stadium pass and been delayed by a particularly officious gatekeeper. When the women at last came onto the court, they were booed for tardiness. But if the delay had been long, the match

Wills didn't get a chance to test her steady forehand against Suzanne Lenglen at Paris. Lenglen pleaded illness and stayed away from the Games.

moved fast: Vlasto, one of the last players to serve underhand, was no match for Wills' efficient power. Wills won, 6-2, 6-2.

Suzanne Lenglen appeared in the stands to watch the American's early matches—drawing all eyes to herself. She left in short order, saying the heat made her ill.

Wills returned to America a heroine and settled into college life. But she and Lenglen were bound to meet at some point. The press and public of two continents demanded it—and so, most likely, did their own egos. By January of

Lenglen and Wills shake hands across the net after their epic 1926 match at a tiny Cannes tennis club while an official rushes to hold back frenzied fans and journalists. The dramatic two-set exhibition was the only meeting between the two greatest women tennis players of their era.

1925, Lenglen was back in form. Beginning with the winter season on the Riviera, she moved effortlessly from title to title; it was in this year that she made her sixth Wimbledon win.

As for Wills, she won the Wightman Cup—played in the U.S. in the summer of 1925—as well as the U.S. women's singles championship, beating Kathleen McKane both times. By August of that year, even the staid *New*

Yorker was claiming that only Wills stood a chance against the Frenchwoman.

Helen Wills had to take that chance, and in 1926 she did. In January she sailed with her mother for France, ostensibly to paint. But she had her racquets with her, and she soon traveled to the Riviera—Lenglen territory—where the winter tennis season was just beginning.

Wills went unsponsored by the U.S. Lawn Tennis Association. Instead, she was paid by International News Service to write about tennis. She also did a lively business selling her not very competent drawings and paintings for prices inflated by her fame. But this was not quite professionalism—Wills carefully protected her amateur status—and it was nothing compared with the machinations of the Riviera tennis clubs and of Suzanne Lenglen's father in their efforts to extract every sou of profit from the proposed match.

For weeks, while the press coverage grew ever more outrageous and the clubs maneuvered for the match, the two women played cat-and-mouse. They competed in numerous tournaments—but not against each other. Wills' strong game steadily improved.

The American Girl and the French goddess of the courts finally faced each other on the morning of February 16, at the Carlton Club in Cannes. The crowd of 5,000, fed to frenzy on a constant diet of banner headlines, filled hastily built bleachers, hung in the treetops, peered from the windows and roofs of neighboring houses. This match was not to be missed—not only because of the excellent tennis it promised, but equally for the clash of styles and cultures.

The crowd was not disappointed: The long-awaited confrontation was as great as the most exorbitant hype could have predicted. It was also every bit as bizarre.

Lenglen lost two games in the first set while she assessed the long drives and sharp angles of Wills' game and searched for a weakness. She found it: the American's lack of variety in play. Once Lenglen understood it, she took control of the set, winning 6-3.

In the second set, drawn and raddled under her heavy makeup, the Frenchwoman played as she had never in her life played before. But Wills was younger and healthier. The two women fought it out for 11 games, the last ending with a drive by Wills that was called out. It was over, and Lenglen had won. In the midst of the ensuing pandemonium, the players shook hands, Lenglen's trembling with exhaustion.

But it wasn't over. The umpire forced his way through the crowd to announce that he had *not* called the ball out. The ball was good.

Lenglen was magnificent. She said only, "Then we must go on," and returned to her baseline to serve. She had to wait while angry fans were cleared from the court.

It took her three more games to beat the young American. At the end, engulfed by spectators, covered with flowers, Lenglen burst into sobs. She had been forced to her limit and beyond. As for Wills, she left the court with dignity, almost unnoticed. Later she said there would be other years and other tennis matches.

But not between these two. Lenglen spent some time recovering, and not long afterward, sensing that her peak had passed, she turned professional. She played in exhibitions until 1929, when her domineering father died. Then she designed clothes for a while. Then she ran a tennis school for children. She remained a star—*the* star—mobbed whenever she appeared to watch tennis tournaments. Yet she remained essentially alone, her nerves taut, her health failing. In 1938 she died of the effects of pernicious anemia. She was only 39 years old. At her massive funeral, dozens of athletes followed the cortege. She was awarded the French Legion of Honor posthumously. She was, said her obituary in the *Times* of London, incomparable.

That same year Helen Wills retired from tennis, having won the women's singles championship eight times at Wimbledon and seven at Forest Hills.

Wills' memories of those Paris Games were bright, even 60 years later, when she was the last surviving member of the 1924 U.S. Olympic tennis team. "It was the best team I've ever been on in my life," she said.

"We had so much fun, and it was so pleasant. And of course, I was so very young then."

All the athletes gathered at the Games of that golden summer were in the flower of their youth then. After the closing ceremonies—the flags, the trumpets and anthems—Pierre de Coubertin sped them on their way with a call for the Olympic torch to illuminate forever "an always more ardent, braver, and purer humanity." The fine gathering dispersed, its members leaving Paris for other competitions and other lives. In the decades since, they aged. They died.

Their Paris has changed in those years. The pool at Les Tourelles is still there, but the swimmers of 1924 would not recognize it. Rebuilt, it serves its still-lively, still-polyglot, still-radical Arrondissement as a public pool: In the 1990s you could swim there for only 60 francs. The Vélodrome

The head of the American delegation in Paris, millionaire industrialist Robert M. Thompson, stands before the dignitaries' podium in an early form of the modern Olympic's closing ceremony. Pierre de Coubertin *(left)*, handed out medals to some of the winners at the end of the Games. (Other medalists would wait for their prizes to come in the mail.) The now-familiar event-by-event awards ceremonies would not become standard until Los Angeles 1932.

d'Hiver has vanished, the only sign of its existence a plaque reminding the passerby of its terrible role during the Second World War, when it became a deportation center for French Jews. The stadium at Colombes still exists, and its dingy catacombs, where legendary athletes dressed and rested, still wind under the stands. But the rest of the stadium has been rebuilt following a fire. Its facade is the bright blue and white of the Racing Club de France, which, supported by the city of Paris, runs it as a venue for athletic events. You approach the quarter not through the cobbled streets of 1920s Paris but by a high-speed highway that shoots through the icy towers and cubes, the steel and glass and marble of the giant futuristic development known as La Defense.

Not everything changes. The street by the stadium, where Paavo Nurmi set off for the 10,000-meter run, is still narrow and dusty. A grimy café, with flats above, faces the stadium entrance. From the windows of the flats, old women still peer down at new generations of runners and soccer players, making their way to practice and competition.

And the legacy of the Olympic athletes of Paris 1924 does not change. Even as they aged, even as their records were surpassed and surpassed again, their memories continue to shine as the brave, pure, and ardent flame that Coubertin described. Athletes of each new generation honor them. When, in 1952, Nurmi ran into the Olympic stadium at Helsinki bearing the torch from Olympia, even the Soviet team thronged the sides of the track to see him pass. And at the 1980 Games in Moscow, when Scotsman Alan Wells won the 100-meter race, he was asked whether he had run it for Harold Abrahams, the last Briton to win the coveted gold of the fastest man alive. "No," replied Wells. "This one was for Eric Liddell."

FAREWELLS AND FURORS

Prague was an appropriate setting for Baron Pierre de Coubertin's final address as president of the International Olympic Committee. The city itself, curving splendidly along the banks of the Moldau, was renowned for its medieval castle, its baroque palaces, its theater, and its music. It exemplified the noble style Coubertin loved. So did Prague's 14th-century Town Hall, where the Eighth Olympic Congress convened on May 29, 1925, to hear its leader's farewell. The edifice, with its mosaics, its Oriel Chapel, and its ornate Council Hall, provided the kind of dignified antique grandeur that Coubertin and his colleagues expected: The IOC president was a man with a profound sense of history. He viewed the Olympic movement he had revived—and for 30 years had led—as part of a spiritual continuum flowing from the Golden Age of Greek civilization through what he called Europe's "magnificent and slowly acquired culture" to the modern era.

As he had throughout his career,

Coubertin now invoked his image of classical ideals as they should be manifest in the Olympic movement. He spoke of the individual athletic champion who, in daring the impossible, becomes the inspiration for thousands. He reiterated the role he envisioned for athletics as part of an educational system that unites sport, the sciences, the arts, and the humanities, and so civilizes entire societies. He called for gymnasiums in the classical sense—municipal meeting places open to all "without regard to opinions, beliefs or social rank"—where citizens meet for sport, for the arts, for open discussion and debate.

Against the ideal he set his view of the reality: a world corrupted by the quest for money, by national passions, by fashion, by educational systems degenerating into specialized rather than general instruction, into manias for statistics and numbers and into dull convention.

The Olympic movement could act as a purifying force, Coubertin thought,

Founding Fathers: Pierre de Coubertin (*right*) and Jiri Guth-Jarkovsky, IOC member in Bohemia, Prague 1925

Members of the IOC stand at attention at the Prague Congress. During the series of meetings, the IOC elected a new president, clarified the role of the national Olympic committees, and revised the definition of amateur.

if its size and growing commercialism were controlled, and if sports hierarchies were simplified—and cleansed of mendacity and hypocrisy. Above all, the International Olympic Committee must remain as he had conceived it: independent, self-recruiting, free of nationalism and of financial interest. It must not let itself be infiltrated or corrupted. He himself was leaving now, to pursue his greater goal, "the introduction of a pedagogy productive of mental clarity and critical calm." As for committee members, "they will continue in the same spirit their ascent of the hill on which we hope to raise a temple, while an immense market is organized on the plain. The temple will endure and the market will pass away. Market or temple—sportsmen must make their choice; they cannot expect to frequent both one and the other. Let them choose!"

The speech was more the valediction of an abdicating monarch than of a retiring president of a sports committee. And in truth, by a powerful blending of vision and intelligence, social and familial contacts, and shrewd political maneuvering—not to mention the sacrifice of much of his own considerable fortune—Coubertin had created in the Olympic movement a kind of floating country of his own. He was its king: The president of the IOC had enormous discretionary powers.

His council was the IOC, in the beginning care-

fully selected by him from a vast network of acquaintances. This council would, it is true, eventually grow troublesome, sometimes flouting the king's wishes, seeking in the end to perpetuate itself and choose its own new colleagues. In the early days, though, Coubertin picked his councilors with an eye toward insuring their independence from all influence other than his own: He chose men of his own class and ideals. All were well educated, each distinguished in his own right, all interested in sport, most titled, most rich. These men not only governed according to a charter that Coubertin had devised, they served as ambassadors to the Olympic committees of each nation involved in the Games: An IOC member, it was emphasized, was a member *in* a country, not of or from a country. The IOC also negotiated with the international federations that oversaw each sport—federations whose power would increase significantly as the years went on. To facilitate the IOC's several functions, and to serve in his place during his frequent travels, Coubertin had appointed a six-man Executive Committee—an inner circle, a privy council—in 1921.

This Olympic nation had its own heraldry, its own ritual, and its own calendar. The four-year Olympiads proceeded in a stately round, beginning with the Games, which Coubertin conceived of as a celebration of arts, literature, and sport; a "festival of academic youth," of "supreme effort"; of a transcendent "spring of mankind." The Games—their location and composition—were under the ultimate control of the IOC; local matters related to the Games (the selection of national teams, for example) were handled by the national Olympic committees; technical concerns such as rules and judging were delegated to each sport's governing body, its international federation.

Besides the Games, the calendar included annual Sessions of the IOC, and there might also be a Congress, called at the discretion of the president. A Congress consisted not only of IOC members but also of delegates from national Olympic committees and from the international sports federations. The Games themselves were to be the ultimate expression of the Olympic idea; the Sessions and Congresses were to forward Olympism itself and its educational ideal.

By 1925, however, this complex of concepts and hierarchies had generated issues and problems that were altering the nature of Coubertin's vision. World sport occupied most of the IOC's attention: The movement's educational aspect had receded into the background—if, indeed, it had ever been elsewhere. (The Prague meeting's Pedagogical Congress, held in Coubertin's honor, was to be the last of its kind.) There were tensions between the IOC president and the chairman of his Executive Committee, who acted more independently than the autocratic Coubertin had foreseen; in fact, Coubertin found himself too frequently overridden. It was time for him to move on, as his speech made clear, to the educational issues he believed would determine the future of civilization. For the rest of his life, he would teach, write, and supervise the organizations for sports education that he had established in Switzer-

land. Although the IOC had made him honorary president of the Olympic Games for life, and he would stay in close touch with IOC members, he would never again attend the Games.

His successor as IOC president, elected at Prague, was the vice-chairman of the Executive Committee, Count Henri de Baillet-Latour. A Belgian aristocrat, brought up with his country's king, Baillet-Latour was a diplomat, a noted horseman, and a long-serving member of the IOC, loyal to Coubertin and his beliefs. He had been one of the founders of Belgium's Olympic committee, he had taken Belgian teams to London in 1908 and Stockholm in 1912, and he had presided over the organizing committee for the 1920 Antwerp Games.

Less of a visionary, perhaps more conservative than Coubertin, Baillet-Latour found himself leading an Olympic movement in the process of evolution. Some of the issues at hand in 1925 were philosophical: The IOC, as it was to do for decades, was still wrangling over an anachronistic definition of the amateur athlete. Various political matters—from the definition of the Executive Committee's authority to the question of whether to sponsor Winter Games—required resolution. There were colonizing efforts to consider: Coubertin had long been interested in regional games for nations not part of the Western sports network—but what was to be their function, and what the IOC's role

Attendees of the Eighth Olympic Congress received a commemorative medal, a traditional gift for every meeting. A stylized design of Prague's Hradcany Castle dominates the front of it (left). The Olympic rings and motto adorn the back (below).

107

Belgian Count Henri de Baillet-Latour *(center)*, Pierre de Coubertin's successor as IOC president, gathers with other leaders of the Olympic movement during the 28th IOC Session in Lausanne, Switzerland. Just behind Baillet-Latour and to the right is Sigfrid Edström of Sweden, a future IOC president.

in them? Finally, there were a number of challenges to the lofty authority of the Olympic state. Some came from the international sports federations, pursuing their own agendas and goals. Others arose among groups who saw themselves excluded from Olympia, such as women, or who disapproved of the Olympian approach, such as socialists and communists.

Most of these issues had their deep roots—as did modern sport itself—in the cataclysmic changes wrought by the Industrial Revolution on the 19th-century world. This revolution in farming, industry, transportation, and finance created enormous wealth and, in what William Blake called its "dark Satanic mills," a huge underclass.

Dependent as it was on wretched masses of semi-slaves working at dull, repetitive jobs in the most squalid of conditions, the Industrial Revolution contributed greatly to the waves of political revolt that swept Europe at mid-century. A militant working class began to organize, watched

with varying degrees of anxiety by the privileged. "Society was split in two," wrote the French historian Alexis de Tocqueville. "Those who had nothing united in common envy; those who had anything united in common terror."

The birth of modern sport—"specialized, rationalized, bureaucratically organized and marked by a kind of mania for quantification and the records that quantification makes possible," as historian Allen Guttman put it—is directly linked to these great social changes. Sport emerged in several forms. In Great Britain and America, for instance, athletics was, for the upper classes, part of the training of future rulers, a medium for instilling qualities of leadership. Sport was games, and leaving aside such activities as hunting, it was always competitive: Competition taught cooperation, team spirit, and courage.

But the working classes loved their sports, too. The rationalized industrial system provided, for the first time, a clear division between working time and leisure time. As reformers

became active in industry, which they did very early, workers had more leisure. Their employers set up company sports clubs to diffuse workers' growing militancy and encourage industrial peace. Religion initiated sports programs to bring laborers into the fold: The Young Men's Christian Association and the Young Women's Christian Association were created in the 1880s, the Young Men's Hebrew Association just before World War I. And, workers established their own sports programs just because games were fun; they provided a happy escape from dull work. Sometimes these sports programs were political.

Multiplying clubs of every description—and the sports journalism that expanded with them—created a craze for sport that demanded, in very short order, some kind of regulation and administration: There had to be commonly agreed-upon rules for competition; there had to be ways to organize events profitably; there had to be people to keep records. At this point—beginning roughly in the last quarter of the 19th century—the clubs began to unite in associations and the associations into international federations.

Britain led in this development, and for a large part of this century international sport was shackled by English sporting rules, which were disguised as ideals but were all-too-obvious means of protecting the upper classes' hold on "their" games. Workers might enjoy sporting contests, according to this philosophy, but workers competed for cash prizes. Sometimes they accepted payment for the time they lost from work when competing. In short, their motives were impure. The true sportsman, according to the British definition, was an amateur. Sport was one of the many liberal arts he was familiar with and practiced in his copious amount of spare time.

Perhaps the most repugnant expression of this attitude was to be found in the British Amateur Athletic Club's regulation of 1866, which defined an amateur as "any gentleman who has never competed in an open competition, or for public money, or for admission money, and who has never at any period of his life taught or assisted in the pursuit of athletic exercises as a means of livelihood or is a mechanic, artisan or labourer." This definition was relaxed—some—by the British Amateur Athletic Association in 1880. The prestigious Rowing Federation, however, retained the bar on workers.

That Pierre de Coubertin was by birth and breeding a gentleman himself is beyond question. It is also beyond question that he loathed the idea of sport for gentlemen only. His own interest in sport centered on its value as a shaper of men—on the discipline it offered for mind and body, on the qualities of fairness and leadership that it could instill. Sport was for youth, Coubertin believed—all youth, of all classes, everywhere. Yet in founding the Olympic Games, he allowed the incorporation of an amateur rule, for complex reasons.

Primarily—and ironically—he was concerned with correcting abuses that would fade in time anyway. Chief among them were the savagery and dishonesty that besmirched the professional sports of his day. Professional football games in the United States and rugby games in England degenerated all too often into brutal free-for-alls. Coubertin wanted no such taints on his Olympic Games. A second problem had to do with paying people to take part in contests that were supposed to be amateur. This practice went on virtually everywhere in Coubertin's day, but it was particularly rife in the United States. Student football players at Harvard, say, in their eagerness to win games, might go to Boston's docks and pay a brawny longshoreman a few dollars to join the team. In short, collegians had been known to hire ringers; and ringers, because they played for pay, were professionals. To Coubertin the deceit and unfairness of this activity were antithetical to every good thing he envisioned sport to be: Sport was supposed to strengthen and ennoble young men; this sort of professionalism corrupted them.

As sport became more sophisticated, more organized, and more regulated, ringers would gradually vanish; by the 1930s they would no longer be a problem. Similarly, increased oversight and stricter rules would correct some of the more flagrant abuses in professional sports. A few decades earlier, though, few could have foreseen these happy outcomes. Thus Coubertin, with his own idealistic reasons for protecting amateurism, found himself in uneasy accord with adherents of the British gentlemen-only tradition: All agreed that the Olympic Games should be for amateurs. For the rest of his life, the baron would try to steer the Games on a middle course between classism on one hand and corruption on the other. And, sadly, he would fail.

As always, the devil was in the details and the definitions. Exactly what was an amateur? (That question, destined to plague the IOC for decades, predated even the IOC itself: At the Paris Congress of 1894, the historic meeting that marked the founding of the modern Games, a commission was formed to consider amateurism. So contentious were its deliberations that modern Olympism was almost stillborn.)

Sport for the love of sport, not for gain, seemed a fair part of the Olympic ideal. But what did "financial gain" cover? The possibilities seemed endless, and except for the period during World War I, the IOC from its inception spent interminable hours gathering data, arguing, and revising its regulations. The task was complicated by the IOC's relationship to the international sports federations, and by the fact that those federations had different rules about amateurism for different sports; sometimes international and national federations had different rules for the same sport.

By the time he retired in 1925, Coubertin—who was, as always, pressing for the democratization and the spread of sport—was thoroughly sick of the question. He thought that a sworn oath that an athlete was an amateur should be enough. The IOC clearly didn't agree: It continued to define and redefine the concept of amateur status, seeking to control the many abuses—primarily concealed payment to athletes—endemic in the athletic community.

The Prague Congress' definition entailed some fine points: The IOC termed professional anyone who received part or all of his living from sport; further, anyone who was a professional in one sport could not be an amateur in another. Coaches, trainers, and sports instructors all counted as professional and could neither compete nor judge at the Games. Anyone who received "broken-time" payments—compensation for time lost from work while competing—was professional (although someone who used paid vacation to compete was not). Furthermore, once an athlete became a professional, his amateur status could never be restored. Finally, strict rules were enacted to limit the amount of time an athlete could spend traveling to competitions. Sport historian Karl Lennartz, writing in later, wiser years, would remark that the purpose of the rules was to keep class barriers up: "Anyone who could not afford to practice sport should not do so, or at least not with those ennobled by the status of amateur."

The IOC looked to the sports federations to enforce the amateur rule: Athletes were to be certified by their federations (and the certifications countersigned by their national Olympic committees). But the amateur rules formulated in Prague swiftly led to conflict with those federations.

The International Lawn Tennis Federation (ILTF), for instance, allowed a professional to be reclassified as an amateur under certain conditions. And, as part of a power struggle it was waging with the IOC, it demanded that the Olympic body recognize ILTF amateur rules.

Finnish track star Vilho Ritola, a five-time gold medalist during his Olympic career, plies his trade as a carpenter. Ritola supported himself with a number of blue-collar jobs, as did other great Olympians of his day. Under the IOC's amateur rule, athletes could not market their Olympic fame if they wanted to remain eligible to compete in the Games.

The IOC refused: The only athletes who could compete in the Games were those who conformed to IOC regulations. The federation's response was to forbid its members to participate in the Games, beginning a boycott that would last for decades. Not until Seoul 1988 would tennis rejoin the Olympics as a medal event.

Dissension over the amateur rule was hardening into an Olympic theme, and dealing with it would require continuing and lengthy negotiations, and often compromise. Marksmen, who frequently competed for cash prizes, did not appear at Amsterdam 1928. Four years later in Los Angeles the shooting events were back, but several European teams harbored nonamateurs. The demand for the shooting contests was so great for the 1936

Olympics in Berlin that the IOC backed down on its reinstatement clause and agreed to let marksmen compete if they had taken no cash prizes for two years prior to the Games.

Perhaps the conflict that attracted most attention, however, was that with FIFA (Fédération Internationale de Football Association), the federation for soccer. Soccer had evolved as a working-class sport; most of its players had jobs to do and families to support. In the 1920s there were no laws requiring employers to provide paid holidays: Some did, and some didn't. Players whose companies did not provide holidays could lose money—or even their jobs—if they took time off to compete. In 1926, therefore, FIFA decided that it would equalize opportunities by reimbursing players who got no paid leave, a ruling directly contravening the IOC's.

According to its own laws, the IOC should have demanded that FIFA repeal its decision or leave the Games. But soccer was a crowd pleaser that brought in important income. Furthermore,

Socialism's red banners wave during the opening ceremony of the Vienna Workers' Olympics. The 1931 games marked the high point of the workers' sports movement: Some 80,000 athletes from 23 nations competed.

if not participating in the Games, FIFA might instigate rival world championships. (As sport expanded during these decades, the IOC grew concerned about competition with the Olympic Games. In fact, the 1925 Congress requested that international federations consider the Games their world championships—or at least that they not stage their own in the same years as the Games.) So Baillet-Latour and his Executive Committee worked out a hair-splitting compromise: FIFA would reimburse not play-

ers, but their employers, who could then pass the money on to the players.

This decision permitted soccer competitions in the Amsterdam Games, but it caused an uproar among other federations, national Olympic committees, and within the IOC itself. The furor continued—despite all Baillet-Latour's explanations and negotiations—until 1930. At that time, the IOC ruled that no broken-time payments of any kind could be made within the amateur rules. FIFA immediately withdrew from

Olympic competition. It staged its own world
championships that same year. And the arguments about amateurism dragged on and on.

Among the possible rivals to the Olympic
Games of the 1920s and 1930s were the
international sports festivals staged by
working-class groups allied to political parties.
These were offered as "humanistic" alterna-
tives to what the parties saw as the elitism, international competitiveness, and "excesses" of
the Olympic Games. The Workers' Olympics
attracted hundreds of thousands of people in
1921, 1925, and 1931.

The workers' games were firmly anchored in
ideology. By the last quarter of the 19th century,
labor movements and midcentury revolutionary
thought had coalesced into socialist parties of
varying stripes. All the parties' members believed in Karl Marx's class struggle—capitalists
versus workers. All believed that capitalism
would die and a better world emerge. But the
right wing—which in many nations rapidly became a powerful force for extending the franchise, instituting state welfare benefits, and improving working conditions—thought it could
effect a peaceful transition to the new order.
The left insisted that only violent revolution

Posters for the 1931 and
1937 Workers' Olympiads
illustrate both summer
and winter sports in the
same strong, angular
style. The 1937 festival
in Antwerp was the
last of its kind.

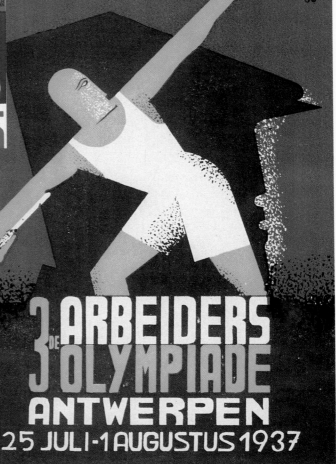

4. Übung

(Pause) 14   13   12   11   9 10   8   7   6   5   4 3 2 1
16 15   (Pause)   (Langsam heben)

Socialist gymnasts perform exercises in a numbered series. At some workers' athletic gatherings, the numbered routines were described in programs handed out to participants before the games.

would overthrow capitalism. The two groups remained in bitter conflict as to how to achieve the final, ideal state—one worldwide and wealthy. There would be no governments, social classes, law, or politics in this socialist utopia. Greed would be eliminated; goods would be distributed according to need.

The history of the 20th century shows the dismal fate of these ideas, and the story of the workers' sports movement faithfully reflects that history. Initially, labor leaders evinced little interest in sport—they had more serious things on their minds—but by the late 19th century, workers' sports societies had emerged throughout the industrialized world, founded to ensure that young people could enjoy healthy outdoor activities in a properly ideological atmosphere, shielded from insidious bourgeois influences. The emphasis—at first—was on less competitive athletics such as hiking and gymnastics.

After World War I the movement became more interested in team sport and competition; the various groups began to unite; a labor sports press developed; and in 1920 at Lucerne, two Belgian organizers created the federation of sporting clubs known first as the Lucerne Sports International (LSI) and later as the Socialist Workers' Sports International. It was to have more than two million members. This was a (comparatively) moderate group: In order to achieve state recognition and funding, its leaders thought it necessary to cooperate with their governments. However, to keep the organizations free of any taint of elitism, the bylaws stated, among other things, that no member of any

of its sports federations could also belong to a bourgeois sports group.

The left-wing rival to the LSI was the Red Sport International (RSI), formed in Moscow in 1921. Its members were not established sports clubs, but small groups of Communists. Its goals, announced with the usual dreary Communist belligerence, were first to take over existing workers' sports groups and then to use them "in the service of the proletarian revolution." A particular target was the Lucerne Sports International, and the means to conquer it was to be the creation of factions—destruction from within. At the same time, Red Sport insisted it wanted a united sports movement.

With a start like this, it's hardly surprising that the short history of the workers' sports movement is one of ugly rhetoric and venomous infighting. The RSI certainly was involved in the Soviet Spartakiads—communism's answer to the Olympic Games—in the 1920s. It also tried to participate in the European sports festivals sponsored by the LSI, but because its concept of participation included anti-LSI, slogan-screeching demonstrations and other disruptive behavior, its members were not popular.

Nevertheless, European workers' games were massive affairs, massively attended, and in general full of good feeling. They included traditional competitive sports, even though the organizers decried the Olympic's emphasis on records and stars, but the proletarian festivals focused on group participation and international fellowship: Everyone could compete and, it seemed, everyone did. Opening ceremonies featured red flags and socialist hymns rather than national flags and anthems, and huge displays and dramatic presentations about socialist ideals abounded.

The first, unofficial workers' festival was staged in Prague in 1921. By 1925 the LSI had organized the first official Workers' Olympics as a festival of peace. It had both winter and summer games. The summer games, at Frankfurt am Main, drew competitors from 19 countries as well as 150,000 spectators. (The RSI, after a series of acrimonious negotiations, was not invited to these games because its constituents were not affiliated with the socialist group; it sent delegates anyway, who attempted without much success to organize hostile demonstrations.) Frankfurt set the style for the 1931 Workers' Sports Festival, whose summer games at Vienna were

the high point of the movement. Invitations were sent out in German, French, Czech, and—with dogged idealism—Esperanto. The program included a children's sports festival, more than 200 different sporting events, a run-and-swim through Vienna, artistic displays with massed choirs and pyramids of people, fireworks, a parade, and group exercises—extremely impressive to the 250,000 spectators and 80,000 competitors from 23 countries.

The two rival workers' groups tried—not very hard, it would seem—to cooperate in smaller, local festivals after Red Vienna, but these failed so utterly that communications simply ceased. As the 1930s progressed, and both socialists and communists came under the iron hand of fascist governments, the two factions managed at last to unite.

Gymnastics demonstrations, such as this one in Leipzig in 1922, show socialist sports' emphasis on the masses, rather than on individual athletes.

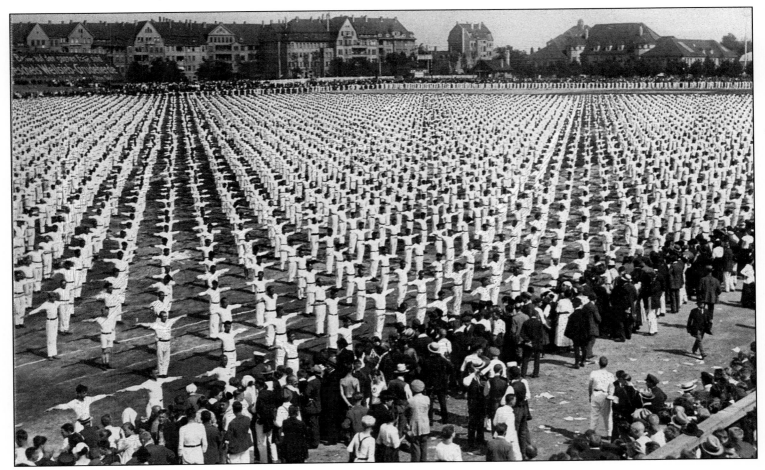

The greatest force in women's sport during the 1920s was France's Alice Milliat. When the IOC continued to exclude women from meaningful participation in the Olympic Games, Milliat organized the Women's Olympics.

They planned a third, huge festival for Barcelona in 1936. On the day scheduled for its opening ceremonies, Francisco Franco's forces staged the military putsch that began the Spanish Civil War. The festival, of course, was canceled. Many of the worker-athletes stayed on in Spain to fight with the ill-starred anti-fascist forces in the war.

Although there would be smaller games after the Barcelona festival was aborted—notably a minor festival in Antwerp in 1937—the workers' sports movement effectively died with the disrupted Barcelona games. Hitler swiftly suppressed its organizations after his rise to power in Germany, and after World War II socialists in

the Western nations were generally content to join the mainstream sports world. The mainstream was becoming more democratic, after all, and it had better facilities, better publicity, and more money than any socialist alternative.

The IOC's attitude toward the workers' sports movement had been a kind of lofty laissez-faire. Coubertin, when he heard about it in 1920, was enthusiastic: He proposed to meet with the workers' unions in a sport-for-the-people congress in 1921. But the IOC apparently wasn't interested. It appointed a commission to study the matter, and nothing more was heard of it. Baillet-Latour, like most people of his age and class, was violently opposed to anything that smacked of bolshevism. In effect, the IOC ignored the workers, except for requesting that they not use the term "Olympic" for their Games, a request that was rejected.

Coubertin may have endorsed the idea of sport for the working classes, but he was rigidly against women competing at the Games—even the limited appearances they had made through 1924—and so were most of his IOC colleagues. But the time came during Baillet-Latour's presidency when the Olympic movement was forced to take women into account.

Coubertin's attitude toward women athletes was typical of the late 19th and early 20th centuries, the period when women's sport developed in schools and clubs. He viewed his Games as "the solemn and periodic exaltation of male athleticism, with internationalism as a base, loyalty as a means, art for its setting, and female applause as a reward." He thought and frequently said that the distortions caused by exertions made women hideous, that athletics might impair the capacity for childbearing, that competition was masculinizing, and that public exhibition by females was vulgar.

Be that as it may, during the early Olympiads—before the IOC had consolidated its power and the national Olympic committees had more authority in organizing their Games—women competed in "appropriate" sports. Appropriate meant sports that were graceful and not too obviously sweaty: variously tennis, golf, archery, ice-skating, fencing, and swimming. There were tasteful exhibitions of gymnastics as well. Even in the memoirs written toward the end of his life, Coubertin mentioned none of the winners of these few events—although he did observe with pride that the IOC had awarded an Olympic medal to a Swedish baroness who had sent six sons as athletes or officials to the Olympics since the Games' inception in 1896.

From the period just before World War I, though, women began to agitate for full inclusion, most particularly in track and field. They were becoming stronger socially and politically, and the work they did during the war gave them confidence. Their interest in sport reflected these changes. France was the leader in this movement. Shortly before the war, when women were refused entry to sports federations, the first women's sports clubs formed, among them Femina-Sport in 1911. In 1917, Femina-Sport sponsored the first national championship in track and field for women. It aroused widespread disapproval, particularly when the public learned that the winner of the shot put, a woman named Violette Gouraud-Moriss, had had her breasts removed in the interest of improving her performance.

These championships, however, inspired a group of women's sports clubs (which, as it happened, were led by sympathetic men) to create the first national women's sports federation. It appeared at the end of 1917. Its treasurer—and by 1919 its president—was Alice Milliat. Milliat, then 35, was a remarkable woman. A childless widow, she was fluent in several languages and earned her living as a translator. But what she really loved was sport—she was a rower—and

Pigtail flying, a British competitor in the Third Women's International meeting, held in Monte Carlo in 1923, nears the landing of her long jump.

from 1919 she devoted her considerable energies to sport for women.

In 1921 the Sporting Club of Monte Carlo staged an international athletic event for women in its little principality—an event whose success occasioned an encore the following year. Inspired by such initiative—and indignant at the IOC's refusal to admit women to all venues of the 1920 Games in Antwerp—Milliat founded the first international federation for women athletes: This was the Fédération Sportive Feminine Internationale (FSFI). The federation immediately began codifying rules for competition and making plans for a four-year cycle of Women's Olympic Games. The first, its ceremonies clearly modeled on those of the IOC's Olympics, was held at Paris in 1922. It was a modest triumph: Sixty-five women from five nations competed in 11 events, with 20,000 people watching. They set 18 world records.

The IOC, always punctilious about the use of the word "Olympic," reacted with predictable outrage. (The activities of feminists in sport were termed "abuse and excess" at the 1923 IOC Session in Rome.) Still, the mandarins of the IOC had their pragmatic side: Since women were obviously entering sport, it was best that they be controlled. To this end, the IOC turned the problem over to the International Amateur Athletic Federation, the governing body for track and field. In 1924 the IAAF voted to admit women, announced that it would govern their athletics, and declared that women's track and field had no place in the Olympic Games.

Milliat's objections to this high-handed maneuver were so forceful that the IAAF was compelled to open negotiations with her organization. It took the groups two years to agree that

British athletes take the lead in the 65-meter hurdles. The British team was a powerhouse at the Monte Carlo games. Its athletes won seven of the 11 events on the program.

the FSFI would remain the independent federation for women but would abide by the IAAF's technical rules, that the FSFI would not call its competitions "Olympic," and that the IAAF would propose that the IOC include five women's track and field events in its Games.

The compromise pleased no one. When the IAAF met with Baillet-Latour and two members of his Executive Committee in 1926, the hot-tempered debate over the proposal to admit women to meaningful Olympic competition was ended only by another compromise: Women's track and field events would be included at Amsterdam 1928 "on a trial basis." The concession didn't sound particularly drastic, but in effect it signaled the collapse of the ramparts of men-only Olympism. (The debris, of course, would continue to be troublesome for years.) Its land-

mark victory notwithstanding, the FSFI naturally considered five events too few, and some members thought women should boycott the Games. The matter was left up to individual members, and, in fact, the British women—the strongest team—did boycott Amsterdam 1928.

The decade that followed produced three more spectacular World Women's Games, as the festival was now called—at Göteborg, Sweden, in 1926; Prague in 1930; and London in 1934. In addition, Milliat created nine different international conferences on women's sports, held throughout Europe: She made the FSFI a force to be reckoned with.

But those 10 years also provided the sorry spectacle of continued power struggles among the FSFI, the IAAF, some national federations, and the IOC. Women—except for the British—did

Women's sports clubs in France organized soccer tournaments.

compete in the five events allowed in 1928. In the 800-meter race, however, three competitors (not the "eleven wretched women" hysterically reported by the *New York Times*) threw themselves to the track in exhaustion, just as men often did. Two competitors from this same race would go on the next day to break world records in relay races, but the damage was done. The public outcry was such that the IOC's Executive Committee recommended in 1929 that all track events for women be excluded from the next Games, Los Angeles 1932. (Baillet-Latour commented that only "aesthetic" sports should be allowed.)

At this point, Gustavus Kirby, an American member of the IAAF, made a stand: He threatened to withdraw the American men's team from the 1932 Games—Games to be held in America—if women were excluded. (Kirby's posture was laudably brave, if inspired by personal motives: His only child, a daughter, was a talented equestrian, and he appreciated her passion to compete internationally.) He had good support, and in 1930 the IOC voted to include women's track and field at Los Angeles, along with women's gymnastics, swimming, ice-skating, and fencing. In retrospect, any decision to the contrary would have been particularly unfortunate: Los Angeles 1932 would see the advent in track and field of America's Mildred "Babe" Didriksen, one of the greatest female athletes of all time.

But the Los Angeles Games still denied

Japanese sumo wrestlers had their female counterparts.

women a full program, and negotiations between Milliat's organization and the IAAF continued. During these, the mighty IAAF moved again to take control of women's athletics. Reports of the next two years' angry negotiations vary so widely that it is difficult to trace the tortuous path of events. But by 1934, although that year's World Women's Games in London were a success, the IAAF was in the position to declare itself the only organization governing international women's athletics and to call for the dissolution of the FSFI. (It did not dissolve, but it did cease to meet.) The IAAF agreed to "do its best" to get the women's Olympic program extended. There were no more World Women's Games: Those Milliat had scheduled for Vienna in 1938 were termed the Women's European Athletics Championships, and they were sponsored by the IAAF.

During these years more and more women competed in the Olympic Games, and the number of events for them slowly grew. To date, there are still fewer Olympic events for women than for men. Nevertheless, the Los Angeles Games of 1984 witnessed the opening to women of that most hallowed of men-only events: the marathon. The first women's Olympic marathon signaled at last a parity that the formidable Alice Milliat had helped make possible—if one that she could only have dreamed of.

Ever-vigilant though it was about rivals to its Games, the IOC remained active in promoting organized sport around the world—particularly in locations where games were in their infancy. Working with peripatetic YMCA sports director Elwood S. Brown, Coubertin and Baillet-Latour helped launch regional festivals modeled on the Olympic Games in areas as far apart as China and Central America.

IOC members and their wives pose for a picture at the close of the 1926 Session in Lisbon. During the five days of meetings, the IOC voted to award the Second Olympic Winter Games, scheduled for 1928, to St. Moritz. The delegates also retroactively granted official status of First Olympic Winter Games to the winter festival known as Chamonix 1924.

The first of these was the Far Eastern Games held in Manila in 1913, with the Philippines, China, and Japan participating. By 1927 these Asian games, alternating among Manila, Shanghai, and Tokyo—were occurring every two years.

Elwood Brown was also the motive force behind the creation of the Central American Games, held every four years halfway through the Olympiad. These games began in Mexico City in 1926. South American Games had been attempted in 1922, but they failed because of Catholic hostility to the involvement of the Protestant YMCA. African Games—intended for male amateur athletes "of African origin" with additional competitions for colonists—were scheduled for Alexandria, Egypt, in 1929. But England and France, with colonial interests in Africa, saw to it that the games were aborted, apparently fearing the nationalistic fervor that the festival might foment. Games were planned for Western Asia—India and the Middle East—but the volatile politics in the area defeated the IOC's best efforts.

Meanwhile, Olympism was expanding in another way with the inclusion of winter sports. Some of the early modern Olympics had been subdivided to stretch over several seasons, and some cold-weather sports were included in these Summer Games. A separate cycle for Winter Games had been proposed as early as 1911, but the idea was always defeated by politics within the IOC.

The politics were national and personal. Except for ice-skating, winter sports became international much later than summer ones. They were the province primarily of cold, remote countries. Not until the travel boom that followed World War I did skiing holidays introduce thousands to the delights of snow and ice, effecting agitation for Winter Games. Until then, Scandinavian members of the IOC opposed them, and the IOC president supported the Scandinavians.

In 1900, Viktor Balck of Sweden, a charter member of the IOC and a close friend of Coubertin, had been instrumental in creating the Nordic Games, which he saw as the counterpart to the Olympic Summer Games. The first Nordic Games were held in 1901 near Stockholm, with Sweden, Norway, and Denmark competing. Thereafter they took place near Stockholm every four years, centered on Nordic skiing but also including bandy, a version of ice hockey; ice-skating; and even fencing and swimming. Although they attracted competitors from other European countries, the Nordic Games were primarily regional—and Balck was determined to protect them as a Scandinavian franchise.

But the Scandinavians met with stronger and stronger pressure after World War I. The Canadians had founded an ice hockey league in 1887; by 1898 they were demonstrating the game in Britain, and 10 years later ice hockey had spread throughout Central Europe. Besides, every nation with an interest in Alpine sports—the Swiss, the Austrians, the Italians, the French—had seen those sports boom just before and after the war. At the 1921 IOC Session in Lausanne, despite Coubertin's attempts to prevent them, these groups established Olympic patronage for a 1924 "Winter Sports Week" in Chamonix. Although it was not part of the Games of the Olympiad, this contest would have most of the accoutrements of an Olympic Games. It would also attract worldwide press attention, which the Nordic Games had never done.

The impressive effect of this event—Coubertin was more than happy to take credit for it after the fact—meant that the attitudes of even the Scandinavian members of the IOC began to change. At Prague, a French proposal for a special cycle of Winter Games, to take place at the end of each Olympiad, won approval. Chamonix was retroactively recognized as the First Winter Games. The second were proposed for 1928. They would be held at St. Moritz.

COLD FEET

Sub-zero temperatures and four feet of snow welcomed the world to St. Moritz the morning of February 11, 1928. Ripped down by falling snow and strong winds, decorations for the opening ceremony lay strewn about the grounds of the Olympic Stadium—if they could be found at all. Roads were clogged with buses stuck in snowdrifts. Organizers had to delay the festival a half-hour to effect repairs.

With all back in order, a hearty crowd of 5,000 watched the small delegations from 25 countries finally begin the Parade of Nations at 10 a.m. The men marched with the tools of their trade: skiers carried boards, while hockey teams came ready with sticks (four games were scheduled for after the ceremony). The women, however, appeared in colorful ethnic costumes that offered a bright contrast to the utilitarian sports garb of the men.

Edmund Schulthess, the Swiss president, opened the Games with a speech which, considering the frosty weather, was mercifully brief. More oratory followed, but to an ever-dwindling audience: Nearly 300 of the 1,200 athletes broke ranks before the ceremony ended, seeking the warm banquet awaiting them at the Kulm Hotel.

THE SNOWS OF YESTERYEAR

ST. MORITZ 1928

When she skated, Sonja Henie once remarked, she commanded distance and gravity: Ice miles ran underneath her blades; the wind split open to let her through; the world whirled around her; speed lifted her from the earth. She didn't have to will herself to move because she flew on the wings of movement itself.

Those who saw this tiny athlete in her prime agreed. Her skating was a lyrical flow of power and grace, luminous, effortless. No one had ever skated the way she did. Henie was one of those rare people—like Johnny Weissmuller or Suzanne Lenglen or Helen Wills—who transformed sport in the 1920s, opening the gates to the realm of the possible.

In early February of 1928, though, as athletes converged on the Swiss resort of St. Moritz, no one yet understood just what the Norwegian child—she was only 15—might do. It was true that she had already won the Norwegian national championship, but her performance at the First Olympic Winter Games at Chamonix in 1924 had been poor: She finished last. She had won the 1927 world figure-skating championship, but the judging had been suspect. Thus few people fully realized what a polished performer she had become. From 1924, Henie's adoring parents had seen to it that their daughter got the finest training money could buy. That was part of the equation that created her. The other part was the iron discipline and the invincible drive of the girl herself.

At the Games' beginning, Henie was only one of 464 young competitors from 25 countries crowding into St. Moritz. Preeminent among them, as in 1924, were athletes from Scandinavia, birthplace of winter sport. These included such skiing legends as Sweden's Per Erik Hedlund, and Ole Hegge, Johan Gröttumsbraten, and Jacob Tullin Thams of Norway. In speed skating, the Finn Clas Thunberg and Norway's

Sonja Henie, April 8, 1912-October 12, 1969. Olympic Gold Medalist, 1928, 1932, 1936

Ivar Ballangrud were the stars, although speed skating was one of the few winter sports in which North Americans were beginning to make their presence felt. (Another exception to Scandinavian mastery was ice hockey, invented and dominated by Canadians.) A New York speed skater named Irving Jaffee would make a mark, of a sort, at these Games. And while the favorite in men's figure skating was Gillis Grafström of Sweden, an artist on ice, the Americans thought they might have a ladies' champion, perhaps in Beatrix Loughran, silver medalist at Chamonix, or in the surprising young Maribel Vinson. Americans, it was believed, would make a good showing in the sledding events, too. The American sledding and toboggan team was thoroughly at home in St. Moritz.

This oldest and most elegant of Alpine resorts both determined and reflected the character of the 1928 Winter Games, not least because of the extraordinarily capricious weather it provided that year: The opening ceremonies, on February 11, took place in a snowstorm. The next two days were also satisfactorily cold and snowy. Then the Föhn began to blow. This wind—famed for the irritability it is said to cause—begins as warm, moist air in the Mediterranean. Cooling and warming again by turns on the Alpine peaks and in the valleys, it blows down northern slopes. When it does this in winter, the Föhn turns ski trails and sled runs to slush, and outdoor ice rinks to standing pools. It blew in 1928 with devastating effects: disruptions, cancellations, postponements, peculiar performances.

But the Games still went on, and the mood was generally as sparkling as St. Moritz itself. Like winter sport, the resort had long been the province of the most privileged of Europeans—and, like winter sport, it was beginning to change.

Set at 6,000 feet, high above a lake in the eastern region of the Swiss Alps known as the Engadine, St. Moritz had been a retreat at least since the 15th century, when pilgrims came to bathe in the mineral springs by the village. The place began to gather international renown in the 19th century, as physicians—believing that pure mountain air would cure the tuberculosis then endemic in Europe—established sanitariums in the Alps. St. Moritz was perfect for wealthy sufferers: The northwest slope where it lay was sheltered from the winds, and it was a suntrap. Even in the depths of winter, geraniums, marigolds, and roses tumbled from village window boxes; and in the sunshine no one needed an overcoat, although the streets were snow-covered and the lake frozen. In January one could lunch on the terraces of newly established hotels or lie in the sun and read. A recovering patient could skate on the lake or ride in a sleigh. And, as a number of invalids discovered, they could also toboggan, adapting Swiss work sleds for running down snowy mountain roads.

It was not long before winter visitors—most of them British and American—began holding races, refining the sleds for speed and building runs with steep twists, curves, and bumps for even more speed. By century's end they had produced the five- or four-man bobsled, ridden sitting up, as the old Swiss sleds had been, with steering mechanisms and brakes. They had also developed the skeleton, a one-person sled ridden lying down, face forward, and steered by shifting the weight and dragging the feet. The skeleton provided a much faster, much more dangerous ride than the bobsled. A series of regular visitors to St. Moritz ensured that it did by carefully developing an almost-mile-long ice tunnel stretching from above St. Moritz's first hotel, the Kulm, almost to the village of Cresta. This terrifying structure, with its corners, banks, and curves and its 515-foot (157-meter) vertical drop, is the famed Cresta Run. It's possible to travel 78 miles per hour (125 kilometers an hour) on it. Every winter since 1885 the ice tunnel has been the site of a race known as the Grand National. The

WHERE THE GAMES WERE PLAYED

Kulm Hotel Ice Rink

Olympic Ski Jump

Olympic Ice Stadium

THE GAMES AT A GLANCE

	FEBRUARY 11	FEBRUARY 12	FEBRUARY 13	FEBRUARY 14	FEBRUARY 15	FEBRUARY 16	FEBRUARY 17	FEBRUARY 18	FEBRUARY 19
OPENING CEREMONY	■								
BOBSLED								■	
CROSS-COUNTRY SKIING				■			■	■	
FIGURE SKATING				■		■	■	■	■
ICE HOCKEY	■	■	■			■	■	■	■
SKELETON							■		
SKI JUMPING								■	
SPEED SKATING			■	■					
CLOSING CEREMONIES									■
DEMONSTRATION SPORT									
MILITARY SKI RACE		■							

Cresta Run is a hallmark of St. Moritz. No other resort has a course to match it.

The men who had this legendary run constructed were generally grand Victorians who for various reasons, including their health, put their energies into sport instead of empire building. They led pleasant, if rather aimless, lives at their country houses in the spring and in London during the summer season. In the autumn they stayed at estates in the north of England and in Scotland for the shooting. And from November to April, they lived in St. Moritz, indulging in its intrigues and its rivalries with other resorts—notably Davos—and refining its Cresta Run. Not that tobogganing was the only sport they enjoyed. By the turn of the century there were competitions in ice-skating, curling, and bandy, and people were experimenting with skis. The first ski-jumping contest was held in the winter of 1904.

St. Moritz was coming into wider fashion, for those who could afford it. And it remained in fashion—if in a slightly different style—after World War I. Fewer people spent entire winters there because fewer people had the leisure. But more people came. To amuse them there were public and private skating rinks, ski runs, and ski jumps. There was even skijöring on the ice, with ski-clad competitors pulled by horses. To house the influx of visitors, new hotels went up and old ones expanded. The three most famous were the Kulm, the Palace, and the Suvretta. The Kulm boasted hundreds of rooms, vast collections of paintings and antiques, and trophy-lined corridors. This was the place where true sportsmen stayed. The Palace attracted the international smart set, and the Suvretta was for families.

St. Moritz enchanted journalists. Writing in the American magazine *Travel* shortly after the 1928 Games, a man named Charles Graves pointed out that snow at the resort—unlike that of London—sparkled. "Every foot of surface glistens like a million diamonds," he rhapsodized. "The fir trees are festooned in white. Frozen waterfalls spout motionless from the hillside; the voluptuous notes of a Viennese waltz played by an orchestra on the nearby skating rink swing up to you lazily; incredibly small Swiss children skid swiftly by on tiny skis; the air is like iced champagne."

Graves observed that most visitors were German, English, or American. The Germans, well bundled up against the winter, watched stolidly as everyone else skied, played ice hockey, sleighed, and—from four o'clock onward—drank, danced, and gambled. This frolicsome lot holidayed in very pleasant luxury, in a place with its own style and its own rules: Those who knew the ins and outs never wore overcoats during the day; it was said to be too

Horse-drawn sleighs (*right*) were the favored form of transport during the eight days St. Moritz played host to the Olympic contests.

The venerable, family-owned Kulm Hotel, shown in all of its wintery splendor, provided quarters for more affluent sportsmen and officials.

The Swiss military patrol team *(left)* receives congratulations for a third-place finish.

Barrel-jumping exhibitions were a crowd pleaser at St. Moritz.

Skijöring racers steer their steeds across frozen Lake St. Moritz.

DEMONSTRATIONS AND EXHIBITIONS

The Olympic Charter allows organizers to schedule demonstration events at every Games. These exhibitions give the host country a chance to showcase its unique sports, commending them to other cultures—and perhaps to Olympic officials for possible inclusion as medal events in future Games. St. Moritz decided on a military ski patrol race. A precursor to the biathlon, the military patrol was a team cross-country race covering 28 kilometers. Each team consisted of four athletes who carried rifles and wore full field packs. Unlike the biathlon, the military patrol had no test of marksmanship. Nine countries participated in the exhibition. The Swiss had high hopes of winning, but the Norwegians proved they were the best long-distance skiers—with or without packs. Switzerland finished third, behind Finland.

While the military patrol had quasi-official status, many other games played in and around St. Moritz during the winter festival did not; they were merely pleasant pastimes for the amusement of players and spectators. One afternoon's events featured acrobatic skating, where daredevils jumped over barrels. The top performer cleared 10 of them. Curling, an icy form of shuffleboard, had its adherents. But the most unusual display was the skijöring contests, which paired the unlikely combination of horse racing and skiing. Lake St. Moritz, frozen solid, served as the racetrack. Hundreds gathered by the lake's edge to watch as horses pulled racers around a circuit. There were no medals for the champion skijörers or acrobats. Winners had to be satisfied with cash prizes.

At the 1923 International Skating Union Championships at Oslo, 10-year-old Sonja Henie shows the developing form that would one day make her a legend. Her first skating title, however, was four years away.

warm in the sun. They always wore red or yellow berets; other headgear was too citified. All these bright young people lent St. Moritz a special hectic gaiety. It was the perfect setting for Sonja Henie.

It would be hard to imagine a childhood more golden than Henie's. Born in Oslo in 1912, she was the second child and treasured only daughter of a couple determined to give her everything her heart desired. They had the means to do it. The mother's family had grown rich in timber shipping, the father's in fur, and the father ensured that his riches multiplied. Wilhelm Henie was a shrewd businessman. He was also a fine athlete—a world champion cyclist, an excellent speed skater, and a skilled cross-country skier. He lived an ostentatiously good life in a palatial house in Oslo, a winter hunting lodge in the mountains, and a 5,000-acre summer estate by the sea. The

Henies had the first automobile and the first private plane ever seen in Oslo.

Nothing but the best would do for their daughter. When, at two years, she showed promise in her dancing classes, her parents took her to Anna Pavlova of the Ballets Russe de Monte Carlo, the greatest ballerina in the world. Pavlova obligingly said the child should study ballet, so the parents sent her to Love Krohn, one of the prima's own teachers. Shortly afterward, during the family's winter holidays, the little girl learned to ski. In this endeavor she was, of course, given the best instructors Norway could offer. A natural athlete, she also learned to ice-skate at the age of five. Because she loved the sport and because it soon was clear that she had the skill and the drive to excel in it, the entire Henie household reorganized itself around her new pursuit. For the rest of their lives, Sonja Henie was the star; her parents, and sometimes her brother, remained her entourage. This was nothing like the child-driving manipulation of Suzanne Lenglen's parents. The Henies, if anything, were daughter-driven.

Such privileged treatment did little for her character: By all accounts, Sonja Henie grew up to be a monster of selfishness, completely incapable of imagining any needs but her own. On the other hand, her parents' all-embracing love and support gave her the concentration and patience her long training required—as well as the confidence and the unfettered imagination that allowed her to reinvent her sport. It needed reinventing: It had become rigidly conventionalized and academic by the 1920s.

Ice-skating has a long lineage. Even in prehistoric times, people moved across the ice using animal bones for blades. The word "skate," in fact, derives from a Dutch term meaning "animal bone" or "shank bone." By the 13th century, people on the Continent—notably the Dutch— were skating, and racing, for pleasure on their lakes and canals. By the 18th century, skating was

well established in France and Germany, as well as in Britain: The first skating club was founded in Edinburgh in 1742.

Like all sports, ice-skating began to assume its modern forms in the 19th century, and these forms were organized and regulated by an international federation in 1892, well before other winter athletics—and, for that matter, four years before the revival of the Olympic Games. Speed skating remained a straightforward racing competition. Figure skating, a recreation of the privileged, was not so simple. The figure-skating blade, unlike the flat speed-skating blade, is concave, with an inside (nearer-the-body) edge and an outside edge, either of which can be used— by those expert enough—to trace large, curving figures on the ice.

As these figures were elaborated in the clubs of London, Vienna, and St. Petersburg during the 19th century, they became highly formalized and fiendishly difficult. By the time Sonja Henie began to compete, the International Skating Union had defined 41 "school" figures, all based on the pattern of a two- or three-lobed figure. Almost all the figures could be performed on either blade edge, making 80 possible test figures. Each had to be performed from a standing start, the figure traced perfectly on one skate, and then perfectly retraced twice more. A competing skater had to master all the figures because he did not know until he stepped onto the ice which six he would be given to perform—and performance of the school figures counted for two-thirds of his total performance score.

Figures, though academic and slow, were the basis of all the free-skating moves that determined the rest of a competitor's ranking: Mastering them gave the skater the control needed for

Gliding across the ice, Henie displays a champion's confidence and style. Her balletic free-skate routine, with fluid moves before and after jumps, made her a near-unanimous choice for the gold medal in St. Moritz.

Judges watch closely as an athlete traces a figure during the skating competition. Compulsories counted for 60 percent of an individual's score. Skaters had to form three different patterns with each skate.

spirals, jumps, and spins—the ballet on ice that lends figure skating its enchantment. Stylish free skating had appeared in Europe in the 1860s and 1870s, when an American named Jackson Haines toured England, Scandinavia, Russia, and parts of the Austro-Hungarian Empire with a program of mazurkas, waltzes, marches, and quadrilles. The idea delighted skaters and audiences alike, and late in the century such legendary skaters as Ulrich Salchow and Axel Paulsen added ever-more-difficult jumps to their free-skating programs. Nevertheless, in formal competitions the monotonous school figures remained paramount.

If the skater happened to be a woman, she was weighed down by more than the tedious compulsory figures. Conventions governing ladylike behavior decreed that she wear long skirts and voluminous petticoats that made jumping dangerous, not to say impossible. The result was unadventurous free-skating programs that were sedate series of unconnected school figures and modest jumps and spins.

Sonja Henie changed all that. She first attracted attention skating as a small child at Oslo's Frogner Stadium. A leading Norwegian amateur named Hjordis Olsen had taught her some simple routines, and these, performed with an athlete's strength and a dancer's grace, had a distinctive

elfin charm. The performances quickly catapulted Henie into senior competition and a rigorous training program. By the time she was nine, she was Norwegian national figure-skating champion and was beginning the peripatetic rounds of international competition. At 11, her Olympic debut at Chamonix caused a sensation. Because she was only a child, she was permitted to compete in the short skirts considered immodest for women. Cute and unencumbered, she dazzled the crowd with some jumps and spins that were, for their time, spectacular.

Still, Henie was not yet ready for Olympic competition: She was no match for adults in the all-important school figures, and her four-minute free-skating program was in some respects a disaster. She had no routine; instead, she executed a move, skated to the sidelines to ask her father what to do next, and executed another move, continuing until the bell signaled her time was up. She came in last, but she had learned.

She knew now what she needed, and her family saw that she got it. The next four years were taken up with training and practice, exhibition skating, competition, and planning. Henie saw Pavlova again in London, learning from the great ballerina how to choreograph a program that gave shape and meaning to movement on ice, a program with a strong beginning and end,

with jumps and spins woven together by dance steps and spirals. So perfect was her technique that she seemed to have none: She appeared to dance for the pleasure of it. Her costumes remained short and extravagant affairs of delicate fur-trimmed silk velvet in pretty colors. Journalists took to calling her "the Ice Fairy."

Henie started to look like a serious Olympic contender in 1927 when she won the world championship in Oslo, beating Herma Planck-Szabo of Austria, the gold medalist at Chamonix. But it was not a clean victory: Of five judges, two—a German and an Austrian—voted for Planck-Szabo. The other three—all Norwegian—voted for Sonja Henie. The ensuing controversy caused the International Skating Union to instigate a one-judge-per-country rule for international contests. It also sent Henie to St. Moritz with something to prove.

She faced serious, experienced competition. Planck-Szabo did not appear at the Games, but

another Austrian, Fritzi Burger, was on the schedule, and the Austrians were famed for their figure-skating skill. Among the rest of the field of 20 was the formidable U.S. and North American champion—and Olympic silver medalist in 1924—Beatrix Loughran, as well as America's Maribel Vinson, a skater not much older than Henie, who had been producing some remarkable performances.

None of the contestants was helped by the weather. The thaws that set in early in the week wrecked the skating schedules—the women's competition was postponed for two days—and when a freeze finally descended and the ice at the Kulm Hotel's outdoor rink was pronounced passable, it was only that. The rink was an obstacle course, strewn with at least a dozen flags that marked holes or ruts. Competitors simply had to skate around them.

It was obvious right away that Henie's costumes had started a trend. As Joel B. Liberman,

Austrian skater Fritzi Burger tries to avoid flag-marked flaws in the ice on the Kulm Hotel rink. Warm weather and damage caused by the ice hockey tournament combined to turn the ice into a rutted, slushy bog for the figure skaters.

Lifts like this one were a minor part of the routine of pairs champions Pierre Brunet and Andrée Joly. The French couple impressed judges mostly with their shadow-like synchrony. Brunet and Joly would marry before winning a second gold medal at Lake Placid 1932.

an American judge, rather stuffily noted, "There was a radical change in the costumes worn by the women skaters, as the modern European woman skater dresses very much as though appearing in a sports number in a musical revue. Most of the girls wear brilliant and daring colors with skirts which can be more accurately described as 'tunics' rather than skirts. Most of the American girls from the point of view of costume were not in the picture at all, with their conventional black skating dresses."

Pert, trim, and blonde, Henie was a standout for looks alone; but the competition would soon learn that she was far more than just another pretty face. Gone was the awkwardness of 1924. Now, her school figures were so finely traced that she had an almost unbeatable lead before the exhibition skating even began.

And if her school figures were good, Henie's free-skating program was uncanny. Only five feet two inches tall, dressed in the briefest and most translucent of pale green velvets, the little Norwegian drew gasps. She was fast: Her music, played by a rinkside orchestra and broadcast through faulty loudspeakers, was a Charleston. Her dance had a shape to it, one that took advantage of the entire space she had, and included pirouettes—some with 80 revolutions—original leaps from the pirouettes, and the repertory of jumps and spins with famous names: axels, salchows, loops, waltz jumps. Everything fitted together; everything was done at speed and with enormous ease and gusto. Six of the seven judges put her in first place; the only demur came from America's Liberman, who voted for his compatriot, Beatrix Loughran. Loughran took the bronze; the silver medal went to Austria's Fritzi Burger.

There were other famous figure skaters in 1928: Conservative, elegant Gillis Grafström of Sweden won the second of his three Olympic golds in the men's singles; Andrée Joly and Pierre Brunet of France, who would go

on to found one of the most prestigious figure-skating schools in the world, took the prize for the pairs. But none lit up the firmament at St. Moritz the way Sonja Henie did. Wearing pink carnations sent by the king of Norway, she led the Olympic Ball, held amid the splendors of the Palace Hotel.

That was the beginning of decades of stardom, kept sparkling by hard work, careful publicity, selfless support from her mother, and clever management—first by Wilhelm Henie, then by Sonja herself. She remained an amateur until 1937, by which time she had won 10 consecutive world titles, six European titles, and three Olympic golds. By that time, too, she was an international celebrity, mobbed wherever she went. And, if even a fraction of the rumors are correct, she was the richest amateur in sport. Her father had seen to it that she collected a considerable amount of money under the table for exhibitions, competition expenses, and the like.

Henie seems to have made only one serious misjudgment in her ascent, and she turned even that to some advantage: She openly courted the favor of Adolf Hitler. In 1935 at a figure-skating exhibition in Berlin, she chose to begin her program by skating at full speed to the box where he sat, coming to a dramatic halt, and giving a full-voiced Nazi salute. Delighted by this little Aryan pet, the Führer blew her a kiss. He telephoned to wish her luck before her Olympic contest, and after it he invited her to lunch at his mountain aerie at Berchtesgaden. He gave her a fondly signed photograph of himself in a silver frame, which she displayed prominently in the Henies' Oslo house, along with a similarly signed memento from Mussolini. Norwegians thought—and said, and wrote—that she had disgraced herself. Their feelings about her remained bitter, especially after Germany invaded Norway in 1940, set up a puppet government, and conducted savage reprisals against the courageous Norwegian Resistance. It was said

An ice skater revels amid snowflakes on the front of the St. Moritz winner's medal. The obverse contains the city name and the Olympiad number, framed by olive branches and the Olympic rings. A diploma *(right)* accompanied prizes for the winners.

that the presence of the framed photographs saved the Henie house from Nazi expropriation in those dismal days.

By then, however, the star had left Norway behind. Henie had an excellent sense of timing. The figure-skating revolution she inspired had produced a constellation of new young challengers who were improving rapidly, and after Berlin 1936 she retired from amateur skating undefeated at the age of 23. Interested in bigger stardom and more money, she had professional plans.

Aided by her father's business acumen and connections, Henie realized those plans in remarkably short order. The first step was a U.S. exhibition tour in 1936, culminating in Hollywood. There, Wilhelm Henie presented her ice show as a social and charity event that attracted the attention of Darryl F. Zanuck, president of 20th Century-Fox.

This was one the film studios that, during the 1930s and early 1940s, lightened the heart of Depression-weary America with a stream of richly glittering musicals. Its president was Sonja Henie's target: She was determined to become a film star. And by shrewd manipulation and some very hard-headed bargaining, she did: Zanuck signed her to a five-year contract, with star billing and the enormous salary of $125,000 per

film. Then he built films around her, all of them stories of ice-skating Cinderellas.

Henie's acting was wooden at best, and her Norwegian accent was almost impenetrable. But her skating—and the staging of her skating— were breathtaking. Films like *One in a Million*, *Thin Ice*, *My Lucky Star*, *Second Fiddle*, and *Sun Valley Serenade* were smash hits. In between films, she toured with the extravagant Hollywood Ice Review, her own frozen equivalent of Billy Rose's Aquacades. Films and ice shows played off one another, and by 1940 Henie was the third biggest box-office draw in Hollywood, trailing only Shirley Temple and Clark Gable.

The stardom faded during the 1940s, but Henie had built an excellent investment portfolio, as well as a fortune in jewelry and furs. Her private life was less successful, lurching messily through three marriages, numerous affairs, family quarrels and lawsuits, and alcoholism. Toward the end of her life, however, she seemed calmer. With her last husband, a Norwegian businessman who had been her childhood sweetheart, she acquired an art collection and endowed a museum in Oslo to display it. She died of leukemia in 1969, in the midst of planning an ice-show comeback.

Sonja Henie's was not a particularly edifying

tale, after the early Olympic triumphs and hopes. Few people visit the Henie-Onstad Museum, as it is called: The skater's friendship with Hitler is not forgotten in Norway, nor is the fact that she chose to spend her life in America as an American citizen.

Like Johnny Weissmuller, however, Henie had done a remarkable thing: She had transformed a sport and she had shown it to millions. She had innumerable heirs, all of them monuments to her very real athletic accomplishments. Among them was the great Soviet skater Lyudmila Belousova, who, with her husband Oleg Protopopov, won the Olympic gold medal for pairs skating at Innsbruck 1964 and Grenoble 1968. The Russian,

famed for her elegant style, said she had been inspired to skate as a child when she saw a dubbed version of *Sun Valley Serenade.*

Sonja Henie's partner at the Olympic Ball in St. Moritz was Ivar Ballangrud, also of Norway: The Norwegians, who dominated these Games, were particularly honored at the festivities. Ballangrud, with his compatriot Bernt Evensen—and with Clas Thunberg of Finland—swept the speed-skating competitions. In the 500-meter race, Evensen and Thunberg tied for the gold in an Olympic record time of 43.4 seconds; Thunberg won the 1,500, with Evensen second and Ballangrud third; and Ballangrud won

Bernt Evensen (*skating in front*) leans into his championship tuck during the speed-skating competition. The Norwegian won a full complement of medals at St. Moritz: gold in the 500, silver in the 1,500, and bronze in the 5,000.

It was smiles all around after Norway's Ivar Ballangrud won the 5,000-meter speed-skating race. Ballangrud's illustrious Olympic career would peak at Garmisch-Partenkirchen 1936, where he would win three gold medals and one silver.

the 5,000, with Julius Skutnabb of Finland second and Evensen third. (Ballangrud and Thunberg dominated international skating from 1922 to 1939: Between them, they won eight European, nine world, and eight Olympic titles.)

The 10,000-meter race, however, was an American story, and not a very happy one. Speed skating was one of the few winter sports Americans regularly competed in during the early years of the century. Because their racing system differed from Europe's—in America all skaters started together in a pack, while in Europe they raced heats against the clock in pairs—the U.S. team arrived in Europe two months early to practice. Team members entered every speed-skating contest they could find, including the 1928 world championships, and took quite a few

beatings. According to American star Irving Jaffee, though, every time the Americans lost, the Scandinavians took them aside and gave all the advice they could. Jaffee thought the Europeans were great sports.

The advice paid off for Jaffee in St. Moritz. The 10,000-meter race was run on February 15. Most of the top competitors had skated and the day was heating up by the time Jaffee's turn came. He was paired with Bernt Evensen, and the two men matched each other stride for stride for six miles. Then Jaffee pulled out his reserves and beat the Norwegian by a tenth of a second. One more pair skated, but by then the ice had turned to slush, and officials stopped the competition.

Because the few skaters who were left had little chance of beating Jaffee's time—at 18:36.5 it was

the fastest in the race—he thought he had won. So did the Swiss Olympic Committee and the International Olympic Committee, whose Executive Committee declared him the champion. So did the Scandinavians, who left for home, sending a telegram to congratulate Jaffee on his win.

Twelve hours later, the International Skating Union overturned the IOC decision, ruling that the race results were invalid and the race must be rerun. Since there were no skaters around to rerun it, this solution was obviously impossible. A number of protests ensued, including a formal one from the American Olympic Committee, but the ISU stuck by its decision.

So Jaffee left St. Moritz without his gold medal. He was seen off by hundreds of athletes, including a Swiss delegation, whose members relieved their feelings by carrying a banner inscribed, "Jaffee, Winner of the 10,000 Meter Race. Long Live America." The Marquis de Polignac, venerable president of the French Olympic Committee, assuaged his own distress by saying that as far as the French were concerned, Jaffee was the champion. Jaffee himself had to wait until the 1932 Games at Lake Placid to win the 10,000 meters officially—and, at long last, to collect his gold.

North Americans won the sledding, too, even though there were no bobsled runs in North America in 1928. There certainly was no Cresta Run. Lovingly tended and maintained, carefully improved year after year, famous for its vicious turns—among them Church Leap, the Sunny Corner, Battledore, and Shuttlecock—the Cresta Run was unique. And it could be deadly: Two people had been killed on it before the war, and there had been several nasty accidents. Only very good skeleton riders who were familiar with its treacherous curves stood a chance of mastering the Cresta.

But a number of sporting Americans stayed in St. Moritz every year, and one of them, a New York investment banker named Jay O'Brien, was made manager of the U.S. bobsled and skeleton team. O'Brien picked his men from among other St. Moritz habitués who used to drop into the Sunny Bar at the Kulm for elevenses, when sun began to soften the ice on the run. Among them were young William Fiske, a 16-year-old Cambridge student who holidayed in St. Moritz and was both a good bobsledder and an expert on the

The Polish team takes a tumble on one of the high-banked turns of the St. Moritz bobsled run *(above)*. Novices rode the American sled, yet they finished first.

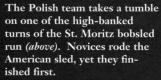

A skeleton racer sliding head-first down the famous Cresta Run *(far right)* takes part in a sport unique to St. Moritz. American brothers John *(left)* and Jennison Heaton, frequent visitors to the resort, knew what gear to pack to help them win the top two places in the skeleton race.

SKI WAX

Athletes have sought a winning edge ever since ski racing began, and ski wax has often provided it. At the turn of the century, little was known about how to make skis glide more easily across the snow. The oldest practice was to burn tar onto the bottom of boards. The hardened tar helped, but it didn't work for all types of snow. Racers tried lard, candle wax, even blood—anything that might do the job. Nothing lasted long enough to make a difference. When Peter Östbye, an unheralded Norwegian, won the prestigious 18-kilometer race at Hollmenkollen in 1914, everyone wanted to know how he managed the upset. The answer was a homemade concoction that he called *klister*—ski paste—and he claimed it was excellent for wet snow. Klister was a blend of beeswax and rubber. Its discovery shook the skiing world. Athletes and coaches set to creating their own mixtures made of wax and rubber with the occasional addition of melted phonograph records. Some shared their discoveries, others did not. Commercial manufacturers had entered the game by the 1920s, but most ski teams still kept their favorite waxing expert on hand. The alchemical pursuit of the perfect wax continues today as skiers maintain their vigil for the ideal compound.

American Rolf Munsen rubs a layer of wax onto his skis at St. Moritz 1928. Then as now, the choice of wax could mean the difference between a medal and finishing out of contention.

Cresta, and Jennison and John Heaton, brothers from New Haven, who spent their summers in Paris and their winters at the resort. O'Brien also recruited a British songwriter named Clifford Grey. Olympic rules on citizenship evidently were less strict in 1928.

That took care of the Cresta, but O'Brien wanted two bobsled teams, preferably of five men each: The rules allowed four- or five-men teams, and the extra weight of the fifth man added speed. So he advertised in the Paris edition of the *New York Herald Tribune*, netting some wealthy Americans who happened to be vacationing in Europe. None of them had ever bobsledded before.

Nevertheless, they put in a fine showing, despite spring-like weather that curtailed the bobsled contest from four runs to two. Fiske, driving

a bobsled called Satan, took the gold; Jennison Heaton, on Hell, the silver. The Heaton brothers won gold and silver on the Cresta Run, defeating Britain's Earl of Northesk, another St. Moritz regular, who was the favorite.

The weather at St. Moritz was no kinder to skiers than to bobsledders or skaters. Still, there were remarkable performances in 1928, in what were then austere trials of endurance, comparable to the marathon in the toll they took on the human body.

Although there were forceful arguments for change at the International Ski Congress—also held that year at St. Moritz—competitive skiing remained in the powerful grip of the people who had invented and dominated it: the Scandinavians. These hardy veterans had only contempt for the showier, more recently evolved versions of the sport.

Their skiing—Nordic skiing—had a heroic past. People had been using skis to traverse the snowy distances of the north for 4,000 years. Viking warrior kings had gone into battle on skis, as did their descendants. By the mid-19th century, people were skiing competitively in Scandinavia, but the sport was primarily limited to cross-country or *langlauf*—long-run—trials. Competitors on hickory runners, using either a classical, diagonal-step style or a faster skating gait, raced long distances across rolling terrain and through deep woods. In some contests they also tried themselves on prepared jumps. The sport required stern conditioning and enormous stamina, and it retained its heroic, military aura.

Nordic skiing came to wide public attention outside Scandinavia at the turn of the century, with the skiing expeditions of polar explorers Fridtjof Nansen and Roald Amundsen. Their courageous Arctic and Antarctic expeditions helped inspire sportsmen to adapt the sport for the Alpine resorts that developed at about this time. Their adaptation was downhill racing: From the top of a course, the skier descended at speeds as fast as 80 miles per hour to the bottom. Or, at slower speeds, people skied slalom, twisting and turning through closely spaced gates. It was dangerous, exhilarating, and addictive. Why waste your time slogging along the valley floor, the Alpine skiers thought, when snow peaks glistened on every side?

Arnold Lunn, Great Britain's pioneer of Alpine techniques, rightly observed in his report on the 1928 Ski Congress that the Scandinavians sneered at downhill racing. They couldn't see their way to changing the international rules to "cater for those who had short holidays among the snows and consequently had

limited opportunities for training." They thought, in short, that Alpine skiing was effete. In any case, they said, all of its techniques were already subsumed in cross-country races. But, as always, the Scandinavians were good sports: They agreed at the conference to institute trial rules for Alpine racing, to observe competitions over the next couple of years, and to revisit the matter at their next Congress, in 1930. (The organization of this sport changed at an extremely deliberate pace: Alpine skiing would have to wait until 1936 at Garmisch-Partenkirchen to become an Olympic event.)

So all the 1928 skiing competitions were Nordic. The first was an exhibition of a military patrol race, in which teams of four in full military gear traversed a 25-kilometer route through woods, up mountains, and down valleys. Norway won, followed by Finnish and Swiss teams.

The most grueling of Nordic races—the 50-kilometer—took place on February 14 under the most bizarre conditions. At 6 a.m. the skiers sat down to a sustaining breakfast of porridge, pancakes, eggs, and ham sandwiches. Swedish lumberjack Per Erik Hedlund had three helpings of everything. Then he had a tremendous argument with one of the Swedish officials about his

Nike, poised on a horse-drawn sleigh, decorates the front of the commemorative medal given to every competitor at St. Moritz. An inscription fills the reverse side.

Slogging through the slushy snow, Sweden's Per Erik Hedlund speeds to victory in the 50-kilometer race. The white uniform he sported for the event caused an uproar within the Swedish camp, but his gold medal turned the jeers to cheers.

clothes: He had chosen to dress in white with a bright red cap, and the national uniform was blue. The dispute was peculiar, but it also seemed academic at the time. The Norwegians and the Finns were favorites for this race.

At 8 a.m. the field of 41 men set off, starting 30 seconds apart. The weather was clear and cold, the thermometer standing at just about 32 degrees Fahrenheit (0 degrees Celsius). Running along the north side of a series of lakes that stretched east from St. Moritz, the course was a brutal test of stamina, with particularly sharp climbs and steep descents.

The test became more severe as the day wore on. The Föhn began to blow and the temperature to climb, turning the snow to slush and then to pools of icy water. By afternoon the temperature had reached 77 degrees Fahrenheit (25 degrees Celsius), creating an almost

intolerable stress on hearts and lungs. Nearly a quarter of the skiers quit.

But the lumberjack Hedlund (still wearing his controversial costume of choice) and his compatriots pushed on, skiing like phantoms and stopping twice to rewax. Unlike the other teams, the Swedes had carried supplies of wax for such eventualities as unexpected warmth. These skiers were also, as Norwegian journalists would ruefully note, in superb condition.

It took Hedlund 4 hours 52 minutes and 3 seconds to win the race—more than an hour longer than the 1924 champion had needed in Chamonix. The sluggish time reflected the terrible conditions. Slow as he was, Hedlund nevertheless finished 13 minutes 27 seconds ahead of his fellow Swede Gustaf Jonsson, the silver medalist. This margin of victory has never been equaled. The bronze medalist was a Swede, too. In honor of

Norway's Johan Gröttumsbraten (No. 26) poses for a picture with American Rolf Munsen (No. 79). Gröttumsbraten could lay claim to the title of top skier at the Games. He won both the Nordic combined and the 18-kilometer cross-country race.

Thullin Thams takes flight in the second of his two ski jumps. The Norwegian soared 239 feet 6 inches (73 meters) down the mountain but couldn't hold his landing.

History does not record the victim of this particular crash at St. Moritz, but dramatic spills such as his were frequent on the controversial jumping hill.

this memorable race and its unflagging hero, Swedish cross-country competitors would wear white uniforms with red caps for every Olympic competition through Innsbruck 1976.

Having lost out to Sweden in the prestigious 50-kilometer cross-country, Norway was determined to dominate everything else. And it did—after a day's delay thanks to yet another bizarre turn in the weather, one of the capricious rainstorms that the Föhn sometimes conjured. The Norwegians won the 18-kilometer race. They also took all three medals in the supreme test of skiing skill, the Nordic combined—an 18-kilometer race and a ski jump. In the ski jump, held on February 18, Norway took the gold and the silver—but the most spectacular performance in the event was that of the defending champion, who ended in 28th place. He, too, was Norwegian. His name was Jacob Thullin Thams.

The jumping hill, the pride of St. Moritz after the Cresta Run, had been built especially for these Games, and it produced controversy between jumpers and judges in both the Nordic combined and the jump. The hill was planned with a fairly long in-run, where jumpers built up speed; a 233-foot (71-meter) slope; and an out-run of 262 feet 6 inches (80 meters). It dismayed the strong Norwegian jumpers: Such a hill is safe for jumps no longer than 213 feet (65 meters), and they wanted the in-run shortened for safety's sake. The world record for ski jumping then was 236 feet (72 meters).

The jump was shortened—but only by less than 10 feet (3 meters) for the individual contest. For this competition, each contestant got two jumps. Thams' first measured a cautious 185 feet 3 inches (56.5 meters). For his second he discarded all caution and went for the record: He hurled himself off the hill with a phenomenal leap and soared like an arrow above the jump course and the valley below. While the crowds watched, breathless, he seemed to hover; then he began the arc of his descent. At 213 feet (65 meters) he was still releasing his landing gear. Sailing beyond the out-run, he hit flat, uneven ground at 239 feet 6 inches (73 meters) and crashed. He was rushed to the hospital, but amazingly, he had suffered no serious injuries.

He was, of course, badly bruised and shaken.

Thams' fall negated his achievement: Low marks on style took him out of the running. The fall gave ammunition to conservatives, who discussed "monster jumps" at length at the International Ski Congress. These new jumps, they said, had only one reason for being: to provide amusement for spectators. They were typical of glitzy places like St. Moritz. Jumps, said the critics, should be limited for safety. The purpose of sport was not to titillate the sedentary public, but to enrich the soul of the athlete.

But Arnold Lunn, who had observed the jump and the fall—he thought he had never seen a

Canadian players pressure the Swedish goal in the finals of the ice hockey tournament. Canada breezed to an 11-0 victory.

Official's badge for St. Moritz 1928.

Perfect weather greets the athletes as they parade onto the Kulm ice rink for the closing ceremony of the Second Olympic Winter Games.

more terrifying fall—took a different view. His was the Olympic view: that sport inspires athlete and viewer together. And, like Pierre de Coubertin, he saw sport in the grandest, bravest terms.

Recalling Hamlet, staring at death and lamenting the fear of it that makes men hesitate to act—and remembering Moses on the mountain, with all the Promised Land of Canaan spread

before him—Lunn wrote, "One returns from seeing Thams jump with a new pride in the race to which one belongs, the human race. The essence of all sport is the duel between the spirit of men and the limitations of matter. A record jump stirs one like noble music. There is the same intangible sense of the finite at war with the infinite, of the unattainable towards which

mankind strives, that undiscovered country whose frontier alone is dimly sighted from the Pisgah heights of high endeavour."

Lunn wrote in the style of his own era. He thought in the innocent, limited ways that dedicated athletes thought during that Golden Age when modern sport was taking form. He had no more idea of the complexities that were coming than he had of another conflict to follow, the one his generation called the Great War. Yet in his innocence, he evoked the spirit that underlies the Games, no matter how politicized, no matter how compromised: the spirit of human endeavor, that restless urge to find new challenges to master, that brave impulse to push the boundaries back.

APPENDIX

CALENDAR OF THE VIII OLYMPIAD
MAY 4, 1924 TO MAY 16, 1928

1924

MAY 4 - JULY 27	**PARIS 1924**
▼	
JUNE 23, 25-28, & JULY 7-12	**23rd Session of the IOC at Paris**
▼	
AUGUST 10-17	1st Summer Games for the Deaf at Paris.
▼	
SEPTEMBER 17-20	Academic Olympiad at Warsaw
▼	
NOVEMBER	4th IOC Executive Board Meeting at Lausanne

1925

JANUARY 31- FEBRUARY 2	1st Workers' Olympic Winter Games at Schreiberhau (Riesengebirger)
▼	
MARCH	5th IOC Executive Board Meeting at Paris
▼	
MAY 17-22	7th Far Eastern Games at Manila
▼	
MAY 24	6th IOC Executive Board Meeting at Prague
▼	
MAY 26-28	**24th Session of the IOC at Prague**
▼	
MAY 26	*At the 24th Session of the IOC in Prague, Baron Pierre de Coubertin (France) and Dr. William Milligan Sloane (USA) submit their resignations as IOC members*

▼	
MAY 28	*Count Henri de Baillet-Latour of Belgium elected 3rd IOC President*
▼	
MAY 29 - JUNE 4	**THE VIII OLYMPIC CONGRESS AT PRAGUE**
▼	
JULY 22-25	1st Workers' Olympic Summer Games at Frankfurt
▼	
NOVEMBER 3-6	7th IOC Executive Board Meeting at Paris

1926

FEBRUARY 6-14	7th Nordic Games at Stockholm
▼	
MARCH 7-8	8th IOC Executive Board Meeting at Paris
▼	
MAY 2-7	**25th Session of the IOC at Lisbon**
▼	
JULY 31-AUGUST 4	9th IOC Executive Board Meeting at The Hague
▼	
AUGUST 27-29	2nd International Women's Games at Gothenburg
▼	
OCTOBER 12- NOVEMBER 12	1st Central American Games at Mexico City
▼	
NOVEMBER 17	*2nd USOC Quadrennial Meeting at Chamber of Commerce Building, Washington, DC*

1927

JANUARY 4-5	10th IOC Executive Board Meeting at Brussels
▼	
APRIL 16-21	1st African Games at Alexandria—canceled
▼	
APRIL 21	11th IOC Executive Board Meeting at Monaco
▼	
APRIL 22-23, 25-27	**26th Session of the IOC at Monaco**
▼	
AUGUST 8	12th IOC Executive Board Meeting at Paris
▼	
AUGUST 28-31	8th Far Eastern Games at Shanghai
▼	
AUGUST 28- SEPTEMBER 4	2nd World University Games at Rome
▼	
OCTOBER 29-31	13th IOC Executive Board Meeting at Lausanne

1928

JANUARY 22-29	1st Academic Winter Games at Cortina d'Ampezzo
▼	
FEBRUARY 11-19	**2ND OLYMPIC WINTER GAMES AT ST. MORITZ**
▼	
FEBRUARY 13-17	14th IOC Executive Board Meeting at St. Moritz

PARIS 1924
7TH OLYMPIC SUMMER GAMES

ATHLETICS (TRACK & FIELD)

Event	Gold	Silver	Bronze	4th–6th	
100 METER	GBR 10.6 HAROLD ABRAHAMS	USA 10.7 JACKSON SCHOLZ	NZL 10.8 ARTHUR PORRITT	4. USA Chester Bowman 5. USA Charley Paddock 6. USA Loren Murchison	10.9 10.9 11.0
200 METER	USA 21.6 JACKSON SCHOLZ	USA 21.7 CHARLEY PADDOCK	GBR 21.9 ERIC LIDDELL	4. USA George Hill 5. USA Bayes Norton 6. GBR Harold Abrahams	22.0 22.0 22.3
400 METER	GBR 47.6 ERIC LIDDELL	USA 48.4 HORATIO FITCH	GBR 48.6 GUY BUTLER	4. USA David Johnson 5. USA John Taylor SUI Joseph Imbach	48.8 NR DNF
800 METER	GBR 1:52.4 DOUGLAS LOWE	SUI 1:52.6 PAUL MARTIN	USA 1:53.0 SCHUYLER ENCK	4. GBR Henry Stallard 5. USA William Richardson 6. USA Ray Dodge	1:53.0 1:53.8 1:54.2
1,500 METER	FIN 3:53.6 PAAVO NURMI	SUI 3:55.0 WILHELM SCHARER	GBR 3:55.6 HENRY STALLARD	4. GBR Douglas Lowe 5. USA Raymond Buker 6. USA Lloyd Hahn	3:57.0 3:58.6 3:59.0
5,000 METER	FIN 14:31.2 PAAVO NURMI	FIN 14:31.4 VILHO RITOLA	SWE 15:01.8 EDVIN WIDE	4. USA John Romig 5. FIN Eino Seppälä 6. GBR Charles Clibbon	15:12.4 15:18.4 15:29.0
10,000 METER	FIN 30:23.2 VILHO RITOLA	SWE 30:55.2 EDVIN WIDE	FIN 31:43.0 EERO BERG	4. FIN Väinö Sipilä 5. GBR Ernest Harper 6. GBR Halland Britton	31:50.2 31:58.0 32:06.0
MARATHON	FIN 2:41:22.6 ALBIN STENROOS	ITA 2:47:19.6 ROMEO BERTINI	USA 2:48:14.0 CLARENCE DE MAR	4. FIN Lauri Halonen 5. GBR Samuel Ferris 6. CHI Miguel Plaza Reyes	2:49:47.4 2:52:26.0 2:52:54.0
110-METER HURDLES	USA 15.0 DANIEL KINSEY	RSA 15.0 SYDNEY ATKINSON	SWE 15.4 STEN PETTERSSON	4. SWE C. Christiernsson 5. USA Karl Anderson 6. USA George Guthrie	15.5 NR DQ
400-METER HURDLES	USA 52.6 F. MORGAN TAYLOR	FIN 53.8 ERIK VILÉN	USA 54.2 IVAN RILEY	4. FRA Georges André 5. USA Charles Brookins 6. GBR F. Jay Blackett	56.2 DQ DQ
3,000-METER STEEPLECHASE	FIN 9:33.6 VILHO RITOLA	FIN 9:44.0 ELIAS KATZ	FRA 9:45.2 PAUL BONTEMPS	4. USA E. Marvin Rick 5. FIN Karl Ebb 6. GBR Evelyn Montague	9:56.4 9:57.6 NR

4 x 100-METER RELAY	USA 41.0 FRANK HUSSEY LOUIS CLARKE LOREN MURCHISON ALF LECONEY	GBR 41.2 HAROLD ABRAHAMS WALTER RANGELEY LANCELOT ROYLE WILLIAM NICHOL	NED 41.8 JACOB BOOT HENRICUS BROOS JAN DE VRIES MARINUS VAN DEN BERGE	4. HUN Gerö/Kurunczy
				    Muskát/Rózsahegyi
				5. FRA Degrelle/Heise
				    Mourlon/Mourlon
				SUI Borner/Hemmi
				    Imbach/Moriaud
					42.0
					
					42.2
					
					DQ

4 x 400-METER RELAY	USA 3:16.0 COMMODORE COCHRAN ALAN HELFFRICH J. OLIVER MACDONALD WILLIAM STEVENSON	SWE 3:17.0 ARTUR SVENSSON ERIK BYLÉHN GUSTAF WEJNARTH NILS ENGDAHL	GBR 3:17.4 EDWARD TOMS GEORGE RENWICK RICHARD RIPLEY GUY BUTLER	4. CAN Aylwin/Christie
				    Johnson/Maynes
				5. FRA Fritz/Féry
				    Galtier/Favaudon
				6. ITA Cominotto/Gargiullo
				    Maffiolini/Facelli
					3:22.8
					
					3:23.4
					
					3:28.0

10,000-METER WALK	ITA 47:49.0 UGO FRIGERIO	GBR 48:37.9 GORDON GOODWIN	RSA 49.08.0 CECIL MCMASTER	4. ITA Donato Pavesi 5. SUI Arthur Tell Schwab 6. GBR Ernest Clarke	49:17.0 49:50.0 49:59.2est
3,000-METER TEAM RACE	FIN 8 PAAVO NURMI VILHO RITOLA ELIAS KATZ	GBR 14 BERNARD MACDONALD HERBERT JOHNSTON GEORGE WEBBER	USA 25 EDWARD KIRBY WILLIAM COX WILLARD TIBBETTS	4. FRA Bontemps/Burtin Mascaux	31
10,000-METER CROSS-COUNTRY, INDIVIDUAL	FIN 32:54.8 PAAVO NURMI	FIN 34:19.4 VILHO RITOLA	USA 35:21.0 EARL JOHNSON	4. GBR Ernest Harper 5. FRA Henri Lauvaux 6. USA Arthur Studenroth	35:45.4 36:44.8 36:45.4

	Gold	Silver	Bronze	4th–6th
10,000-METER CROSS-COUNTRY, TEAM	FIN 11 Paavo Nurmi Vilho Ritola Heikki Liimatainen	USA 14 Earl Johnson Arthur Studenroth August Fager	FRA 20 Henri Lauvaux Gaston Heuet Maurice Norland	
HIGH JUMP	USA 1.98 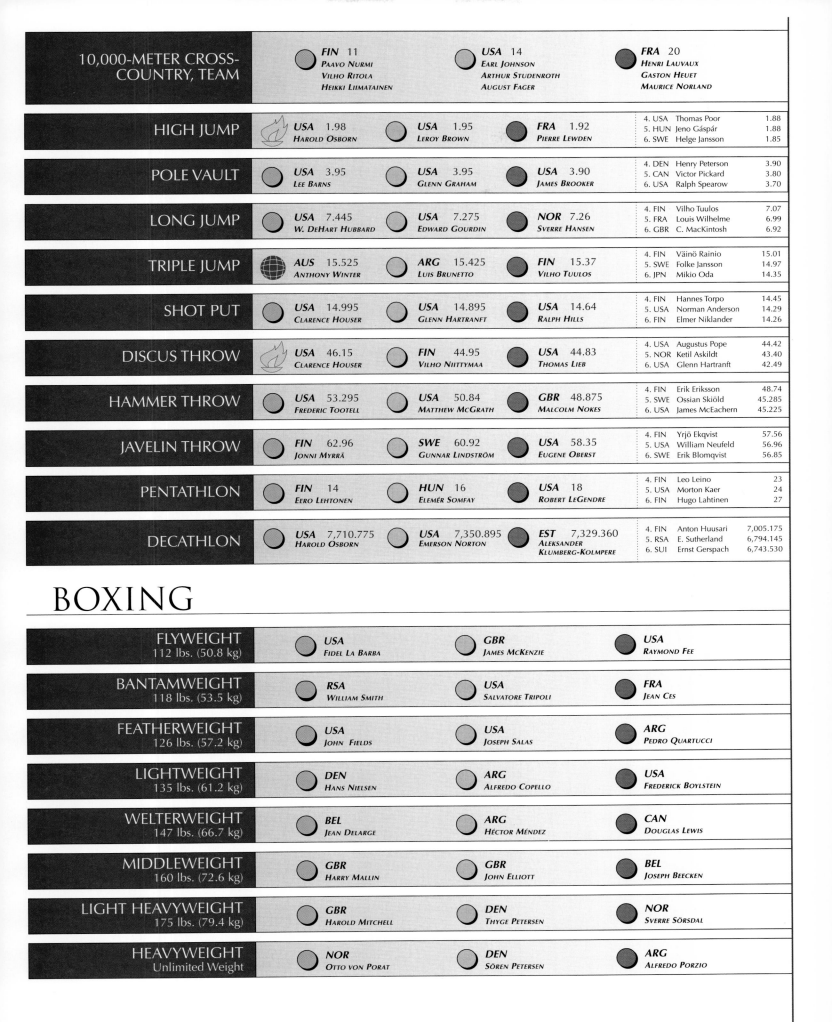 Harold Osborn	USA 1.95 Leroy Brown	FRA 1.92 Pierre Lewden	4. USA Thomas Poor 1.88 5. HUN Jeno Gáspár 1.88 6. SWE Helge Jansson 1.85
POLE VAULT	USA 3.95 Lee Barns	USA 3.95 Glenn Graham	USA 3.90 James Brooker	4. DEN Henry Peterson 3.90 5. CAN Victor Pickard 3.80 6. USA Ralph Spearow 3.70
LONG JUMP	USA 7.445 W. DeHart Hubbard	USA 7.275 Edward Gourdin	NOR 7.26 Sverre Hansen	4. FIN Vilho Tuulos 7.07 5. FRA Louis Wilhelme 6.99 6. GBR C. MacKintosh 6.92
TRIPLE JUMP	AUS 15.525 Anthony Winter	ARG 15.425 Luis Brunetto	FIN 15.37 Vilho Tuulos	4. FIN Väinö Rainio 15.01 5. SWE Folke Jansson 14.97 6. JPN Mikio Oda 14.35
SHOT PUT	USA 14.995 Clarence Houser	USA 14.895 Glenn Hartranft	USA 14.64 Ralph Hills	4. FIN Hannes Torpo 14.45 5. USA Norman Anderson 14.29 6. FIN Elmer Niklander 14.26
DISCUS THROW	USA 46.15 Clarence Houser	FIN 44.95 Vilho Niittymaa	USA 44.83 Thomas Lieb	4. USA Augustus Pope 44.42 5. NOR Ketil Askildt 43.40 6. USA Glenn Hartranft 42.49
HAMMER THROW	USA 53.295 Frederic Tootell	USA 50.84 Matthew McGrath	GBR 48.875 Malcolm Nokes	4. FIN Erik Eriksson 48.74 5. SWE Ossian Skiöld 45.285 6. USA James McEachern 45.225
JAVELIN THROW	FIN 62.96 Jonni Myrrä	SWE 60.92 Gunnar Lindström	USA 58.35 Eugene Oberst	4. FIN Yrjö Ekqvist 57.56 5. USA William Neufeld 56.96 6. SWE Erik Blomqvist 56.85
PENTATHLON	FIN 14 Eero Lehtonen	HUN 16 Elemér Somfay	USA 18 Robert LeGendre	4. FIN Leo Leino 23 5. USA Morton Kaer 24 6. FIN Hugo Lahtinen 27
DECATHLON	USA 7,710.775 Harold Osborn	USA 7,350.895 Emerson Norton	EST 7,329.360 Aleksander Klumberg-Kolmpere	4. FIN Anton Huusari 7,005.175 5. RSA E. Sutherland 6,794.145 6. SUI Ernst Gerspach 6,743.530

BOXING

	Gold	Silver	Bronze
FLYWEIGHT 112 lbs. (50.8 kg)	USA Fidel La Barba	GBR James McKenzie	USA Raymond Fee
BANTAMWEIGHT 118 lbs. (53.5 kg)	RSA William Smith	USA Salvatore Tripoli	FRA Jean Ces
FEATHERWEIGHT 126 lbs. (57.2 kg)	USA John Fields	USA Joseph Salas	ARG Pedro Quartucci
LIGHTWEIGHT 135 lbs. (61.2 kg)	DEN Hans Nielsen	ARG Alfredo Copello	USA Frederick Boylstein
WELTERWEIGHT 147 lbs. (66.7 kg)	BEL Jean Delarge	ARG Héctor Méndez	CAN Douglas Lewis
MIDDLEWEIGHT 160 lbs. (72.6 kg)	GBR Harry Mallin	GBR John Elliott	BEL Joseph Beecken
LIGHT HEAVYWEIGHT 175 lbs. (79.4 kg)	GBR Harold Mitchell	DEN Thyge Petersen	NOR Sverre Sörsdal
HEAVYWEIGHT Unlimited Weight	NOR Otto von Porat	DEN Sören Petersen	ARG Alfredo Porzio

CYCLING

	GOLD	SILVER	BRONZE
1,000-METER SPRINT IN SECONDS	FRA 12.8 Lucien Michard	NED NR Jacob Meijer	FRA NR Jean Cugnot
2,000-METER TANDEM	FRA 12.6 Lucien Choury Jean Cugnot	DEN NR Villy Falck Hansen Edmund Hansen	HOL NR Gerard Bosch van Drakestein Mouritius Peeters
4,000-METER TEAM PURSUIT	ITA 5:15.0 Angelo De Martini Alfredo Dinale Aleardo Menegazzi Francesco Zucchetti	POL NR Józef Lange Jan Lazarski Tomasz Stankiewicz Franciszek Szymczyk	BEL NR Léonard Daghelinckx Henri Hoevenaers Fernand Saive Jean Van den Bosch
50-KILOMETER TRACK RACE	NED 1:18:24.0 Jacobus Willems	GBR NR Cyril Alden	GBR NR Frederick Wyld
INDIVIDUAL ROAD RACE 188 KM	FRA 6:20:48.0 Armand Blanchonnet	BEL 6:30:27.0 Henri Hoevenaers	FRA 6:30:51.6 René Hamel
TEAM ROAD RACE 188 KM	FRA 19:30:14.0 Armand Blanchonnet René Hamel Georges Wambst	BEL 19:46:55.4 Henri Hoevenaers Alphonse Parfondry Jean Van den Bosch	SWE 19:59:41.6 Gunnar Sköld Erik Bohlin Ragnar Malm

DIVING

	GOLD	SILVER	BRONZE
PLAIN HIGH DIVING	AUS 160.0 Richmond Eve	SWE 157.0 Johan Jansson	GBR 158.0 Harold Clarke
PLATFORM DIVING	USA 97.46 Albert White	USA 97.30 David Fall	USA 94.60 Clarence Pinkston
SPRINGBOARD	USA 694.4 Albert White	USA 693.2 Ulise Pete Desjardins	USA 653.0 Clarence Pinkston
PLATFORM DIVING	USA 33.2 Carol Smith	USA 33.4 Elizabeth Becker	SWE 32.8 Hjördis Töpel
SPRINGBOARD	USA 474.5 Elizabeth Becker	USA 460.4 Aileen Riggin	USA 436.4 Caroline Fletcher

EQUESTRIAN

	GOLD	SILVER	BRONZE
THREE-DAY EVENT, INDIVIDUAL	NED 1,976.00 Adolph van der Voort van Zijp	DEN 1,853.50 Frode Kirkebjerg	USA 1,845.50 Sloan Doak
THREE-DAY EVENT, TEAM	NED 5,297.5 Adolph van der Voort van Zijp Charles Pahud de Mortanges Gerard de Kruijff	SWE 4,743.5 Claës König Torsten Sylvan Gustaf Hagelin	ITA 4,512.5 Alberto Lombardi Alessandro Alvisi Emanuele Di Pralorma
DRESSAGE, INDIVIDUAL	SWE 276.4 Ernst Linder	SWE 275.8 Bertil Sandström	FRA 265.8 Xavier Lesage
JUMPING, INDIVIDUAL	SUI 6.00 Alphonse Gemuseus	ITA 8.75 Tommaso Lequio di Assaba	POL 10.00 Adam Królikiewicz

JUMPING, TEAM	SWE 42.25 Åke Thelning Axel Ståhle Åge Lundström	SUI 50.00 Alphonse Gemuseus Werner Stüber Hans Bühler	POR 53.00 Antonio Borges d'Almeida Helder de Souza Martins José Mousinho d'Albuquerque

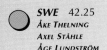

FENCING

ÉPÉE, INDIVIDUAL	BEL Charles Delporte	FRA Roger Ducret	SWE Nils Hellsten
ÉPÉE, TEAM	FRA	BEL	ITA
FOIL, INDIVIDUAL	FRA Roger Ducret	FRA Philippe Cattiau	BEL Maurice Van Damme
FOIL, TEAM	FRA	BEL	HUN
SABER, INDIVIDUAL	HUN Sándor Posta	FRA Roger Ducret	HUN János Garay
SABER, TEAM	ITA	HUN	NED
FOIL, INDIVIDUAL	DEN Ellen Osiier	GBR Gladys Davis	DEN Grete Heckscher

FOOTBALL (SOCCER)

FINAL STANDINGS	URU	SUI	SWE

GYMNASTICS

ALL-AROUND, INDIVIDUAL	YUG 110.340 Leon Štukelj	TCH 110.323 Robert Pražák	TCH 106.930 Bedřich Supčik
ALL-AROUND, TEAM	ITA 839.058	FRA 820.528	SUI 816.661
HORIZONTAL BAR	YUG 19.730 Leon Štukelj	SUI 19.236 Jean Gutweniger	FRA 19.163 André Higelin
HORSE VAULT	USA 9.98 Frank Kriz	TCH 9.97 Jan Koutny	TCH 9.93 Bohumil Mořkovský
PARALLEL BARS	SUI 21.63 August Güttinger	TCH 21.61 Robert Pražák	ITA 21.45 Giorgio Zampori
POMMELED HORSE	SUI 21.23 Josef Wilhelm	SUI 21.13 Jean Gutweniger	SUI 20.73 Antoine Rebetez
RINGS	ITA 21.553 Francesco Martino	TCH 21.483 Robert Pražák	TCH 21.430 Ladislav Vácha
ROPE CLIMBING	TCH 7.2 Bedřich Supčik	FRA 7.4 Albert Séguin	SUI 7.8 August Güttinger TCH 7.8 Ladislav Vácha

SIDE HORSE VAULT	FRA 10.00 Albert Séguin	FRA 9.93 Jean Gounot	FRA 9.93 François Gangloff

MODERN PENTATHLON

INDIVIDUAL	SWE 18 Bo Lindman	SWE 39.5 Gustaf Dyrssen	SWE 45 Bertil Uggla

POLO

FINAL STANDINGS	ARG	USA	GBR

ROWING

SINGLE SCULLS	GBR 7:49.2 Jack Beresford, Jr.	USA 7:54.0 William Gilmore	SUI 8:01.1 Josef Schneider
DOUBLE SCULLS	USA 6:34.0 John Kelly, Sr. Paul Costello	FRA 6:38.0 Marc Detton Jean-Pierre Stock	SUI NR Rudolf Bosshard Heini Thoma
PAIR-OARED SHELL WITHOUT COXSWAIN	NED 8:19.4 Antonie Beijnen Wilhelm Rösingh	FRA 8:21.6 Maurice Bouton Georges Piot	
PAIR-OARED SHELL WITH COXSWAIN	SUI 8:39.0 Edouard Candeveau Alfred Felber Emile Lachapelle (COX)	ITA 8:39.1 Ercole Olgeni Giovanni Scatturin Gino Sopracordevole (COX)	USA NR Leon Butler Harold Wilson Edward Jennings (COX)
FOUR-OARED SHELL WITHOUT COXSWAIN	GBR 7:08.6 Charles Eley James Macnabb Robert Morrison Terence Sanders	CAN 7:18.0 Colin Finlayson Archibald Black George MacKay William Wood	SUI NR Emile Albrecht Alfred Probst Eugen Sigg-Bächthold Hans Walter
FOUR-OARED SHELL WITH COXSWAIN	SUI 7:18.4	FRA 7:21.6	USA NR
EIGHT-OARED SHELL WITH COXSWAIN	USA 6:33.4	CAN 6:49.0	ITA NR

RUGBY FOOTBALL

FINAL STANDINGS	USA	FRA	ROM

SHOOTING

RAPID-FIRE PISTOL	USA 18 Henry Bailey	SWE 18 Vilhelm Carlberg	FIN 18 Lennart Hannelius
FREE RIFLE 3 POSITIONS 300 METERS	USA 95 48 Morris Fisher	USA 95 45 Carl Osburn	DEN 93 Niels Larsen

FREE RIFLE, TEAM 300 METERS	○ USA 676	○ FRA 646	● HAI 646
SMALL-BORE RIFLE	○ FRA 398 PIERRE COQUELIN DE LISLE	○ USA 396 MARCUS DINWIDDIE	● SUI 394 JOSIAS HARTMANN
RUNNING DEER SINGLE SHOT	○ USA 40 JOHN BOLES	○ GBR 39 19 CYRIL MACKWORTH-PRAED	● NOR 39 17 OTTO OLSEN
RUNNING DEER DOUBLE SHOT	○ NOR 76 OLE ANDREAS LILLOE-OLSEN	○ GBR 72 22 CYRIL MACKWORTH-PRAED	● SWE 72 16 ALFRED SWAHN
RUNNING DEER, TEAM SINGLE SHOT	○ NOR 160 OLE ANDREAS LILLOE-OLSEN EINAR LIBERG HARALD NATVIG OTTO OLSEN	○ SWE 154 ALFRED SWAHN FREDRIC LANDELIUS OTTO HULTBERG MAURITZ JOHANSSON	● USA 148 JOHN BOLES WALTER STOKES RAYMOND COULTER DENNIS FENTON
RUNNING DEER, TEAM DOUBLE SHOT	○ GBR 263 CYRIL MACKWORTH-PRAED ALLEN WHITTY HERBERT PERRY PHILIP NEAME	○ NOR 262 OLE ANDREAS LILLOE-OLSEN OTTO OLSEN HARALD NATVIG EINAR LIBERG	● SWE 250 ALFRED SWAHN G. MAURITZ JOHANSSON FREDRIC LANDELIUS AXEL EKBLOM
TRAP SHOOTING, INDIVIDUAL	○ HUN 98 GYULA HALASY	○ FIN 98 KONRAD HUBER	● USA 97 FRANK HUGHES
TRAP SHOOTING, TEAM	○ USA 363 FRANK HUGHES SAMUEL SHARMEN WILLIAM SILKWORTH FRED ETCHEN	○ CAN 360 GEORGE BEATTIE JAMES MONTGOMERY SAMUEL VANCE JOHN BLACK	● FIN 360 KONRAD HUBER ROBERT HUBER WERNER EKMAN ROBERT TIKKANEN

SWIMMING

100-METER FREESTYLE	USA 59.0 JOHNNY WEISSMULLER	○ USA 1:01.4 DUKE PAOA KAHANAMOKU	● USA 1:01.8 SAMUEL KAHANAMOKU
400-METER FREESTYLE	USA 5:04.2 JOHNNY WEISSMULLER	○ SWE 5:05.6 ARNE BORG	● AUS 5:06.6 ANDREW CHARLTON
1,500-METER FREESTYLE	AUS 20:06.6 ANDREW CHARLTON	○ SWE 20:41.4 ARNE BORG	● AUS 21:48.4 FRANK BEAUREPAIRE
100-METER BACKSTROKE	USA 1:13.2 WARREN PAOA KEALOHA	○ USA 1:15.4 PAUL WYATT	● HUN 1:17.8 KÁROLY BARTHA
200-METER BREASTSTROKE	○ USA 2:56.6 ROBERT SKELTON	○ BEL 2:59.2 JOSEPH DE COMBE	● USA 3:01.0 WILLIAM KIRSCHBAUM
4 x 200-METER FREESTYLE RELAY	USA 9:53.4 J. WALLACE O'CONNOR HARRISON GLANCY RALPH BREYER JOHNNY WEISSMULLER	○ AUS 10:02.2 MAURICE CHRISTIE ERNEST HENRY FRANK BEAUREPAIRE ANDREW CHARLTON	● SWE 10:06.8 GEORG WERNER ORVAR TROLLE ÅKE BORG ARNE BORG
100-METER FREESTYLE	○ USA 1:12.4 ETHEL LACKIE	○ USA 1:12.8 MARIECHEN WEHSELAU	● USA 1:14.2 GERTRUDE EDERLE
400-METER FREESTYLE	USA 6:02.2 MARTHA NORELIUS	○ USA 6:03.8 HELEN WAINWRIGHT	● USA 6:04.8 GERTRUDE EDERLE
100-METER BACKSTROKE	USA 1:23.2 SYBIL BAUER	○ GBR 1:27.4 PHYLLIS HARDING	● USA 1:28.2 AILEEN RIGGIN
200-METER BREASTSTROKE	○ GBR 3:33.2 LUCY MORTON	○ USA 3:34.0 AGNES GERAGHTY	● GBR 3:35.4 GLADYS CARSON

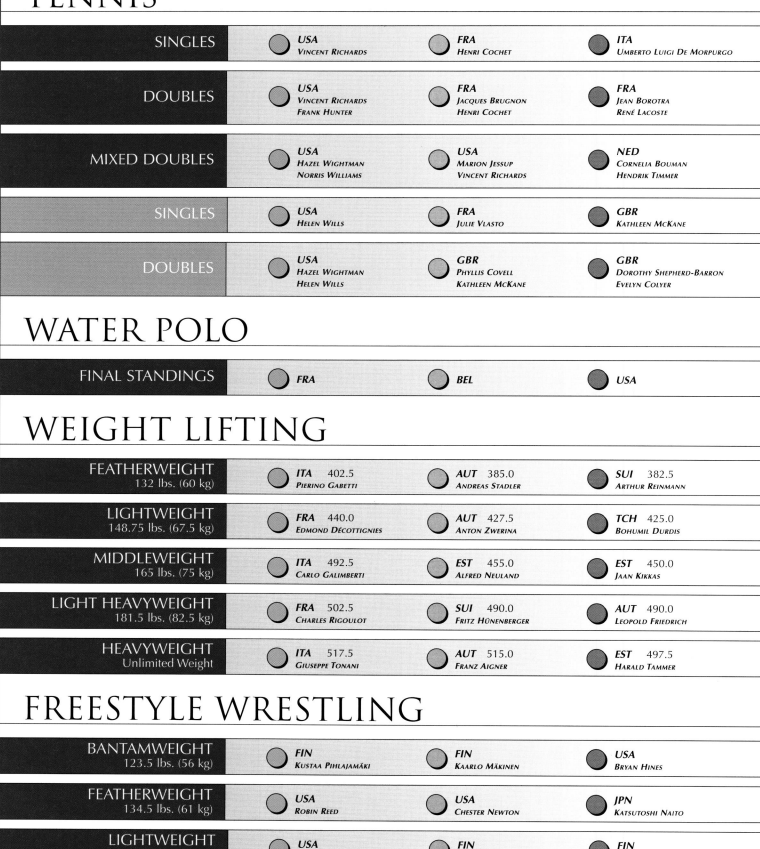

| 4 x 100-METER FREESTYLE RELAY | USA 4:58.8 **Gertrude Ederle** **Euphrasia Donnelly** **Ethel Lackie** **Mariechen Wehselau** | GBR 5:17.0 **Florence Barker** **Grace McKenzie** **Vera Tanner** **Constance Jeans** | SWE 5:35.6 **Aina Berg** **Wivan Pettersson** **Gulli Everlund** **Hjördis Töpel** |

TENNIS

SINGLES	USA **Vincent Richards**	FRA **Henri Cochet**	ITA **Umberto Luigi De Morpurgo**
DOUBLES	USA **Vincent Richards** **Frank Hunter**	FRA **Jacques Brugnon** **Henri Cochet**	FRA **Jean Borotra** **René Lacoste**
MIXED DOUBLES	USA **Hazel Wightman** **Norris Williams**	USA **Marion Jessup** **Vincent Richards**	NED **Cornelia Bouman** **Hendrik Timmer**
SINGLES	USA **Helen Wills**	FRA **Julie Vlasto**	GBR **Kathleen McKane**
DOUBLES	USA **Hazel Wightman** **Helen Wills**	GBR **Phyllis Covell** **Kathleen McKane**	GBR **Dorothy Shepherd-Barron** **Evelyn Colyer**

WATER POLO

| FINAL STANDINGS | FRA | BEL | USA |

WEIGHT LIFTING

FEATHERWEIGHT 132 lbs. (60 kg)	ITA 402.5 **Pierino Gabetti**	AUT 385.0 **Andreas Stadler**	SUI 382.5 **Arthur Reinmann**
LIGHTWEIGHT 148.75 lbs. (67.5 kg)	FRA 440.0 **Edmond Décottignies**	AUT 427.5 **Anton Zwerina**	TCH 425.0 **Bohumil Durdis**
MIDDLEWEIGHT 165 lbs. (75 kg)	ITA 492.5 **Carlo Galimberti**	EST 455.0 **Alfred Neuland**	EST 450.0 **Jaan Kikkas**
LIGHT HEAVYWEIGHT 181.5 lbs. (82.5 kg)	FRA 502.5 **Charles Rigoulot**	SUI 490.0 **Fritz Hünenberger**	AUT 490.0 **Leopold Friedrich**
HEAVYWEIGHT Unlimited Weight	ITA 517.5 **Giuseppe Tonani**	AUT 515.0 **Franz Aigner**	EST 497.5 **Harald Tammer**

FREESTYLE WRESTLING

BANTAMWEIGHT 123.5 lbs. (56 kg)	FIN **Kustaa Pihlajamäki**	FIN **Kaarlo Mäkinen**	USA **Bryan Hines**
FEATHERWEIGHT 134.5 lbs. (61 kg)	USA **Robin Reed**	USA **Chester Newton**	JPN **Katsutoshi Naito**
LIGHTWEIGHT 145.5 lbs. (66 kg)	USA **Russell Vis**	FIN **Volmari Vikström**	FIN **Arvo Haavisto**

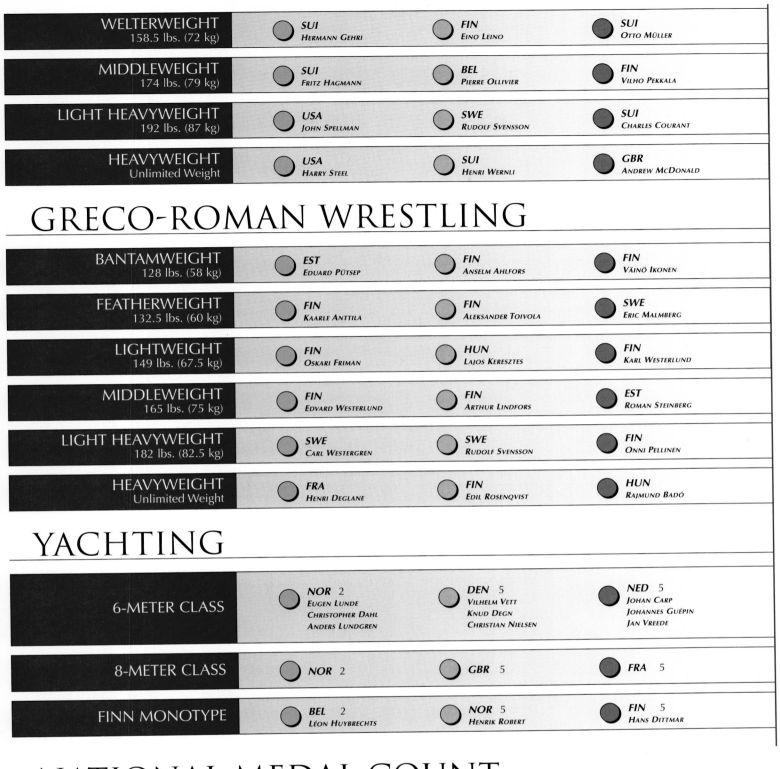

		SUI Hermann Gehri		FIN Eino Leino		SUI Otto Müller
WELTERWEIGHT 158.5 lbs. (72 kg)	○		○		○	
MIDDLEWEIGHT 174 lbs. (79 kg)	○	SUI Fritz Hagmann	○	BEL Pierre Ollivier	○	FIN Vilho Pekkala
LIGHT HEAVYWEIGHT 192 lbs. (87 kg)	○	USA John Spellman	○	SWE Rudolf Svensson	○	SUI Charles Courant
HEAVYWEIGHT Unlimited Weight	○	USA Harry Steel	○	SUI Henri Wernli	○	GBR Andrew McDonald

GRECO-ROMAN WRESTLING

		EST Eduard Pütsep		FIN Anselm Ahlfors		FIN Väinö Ikonen
BANTAMWEIGHT 128 lbs. (58 kg)	○		○		○	
FEATHERWEIGHT 132.5 lbs. (60 kg)	○	FIN Kaarle Anttila	○	FIN Aleksander Toivola	○	SWE Eric Malmberg
LIGHTWEIGHT 149 lbs. (67.5 kg)	○	FIN Oskari Friman	○	HUN Lajos Keresztes	○	FIN Karl Westerlund
MIDDLEWEIGHT 165 lbs. (75 kg)	○	FIN Edvard Westerlund	○	FIN Arthur Lindfors	○	EST Roman Steinberg
LIGHT HEAVYWEIGHT 182 lbs. (82.5 kg)	○	SWE Carl Westergren	○	SWE Rudolf Svensson	○	FIN Onni Pellinen
HEAVYWEIGHT Unlimited Weight	○	FRA Henri Deglane	○	FIN Edil Rosenqvist	○	HUN Rajmund Badó

YACHTING

6-METER CLASS	○	NOR 2 Eugen Lunde Christopher Dahl Anders Lundgren	○	DEN 5 Vilhelm Vett Knud Degn Christian Nielsen	○	NED 5 Johan Carp Johannes Guépin Jan Vreede
8-METER CLASS	○	NOR 2	○	GBR 5	○	FRA 5
FINN MONOTYPE	○	BEL 2 Léon Huybrechts	○	NOR 5 Henrik Robert	○	FIN 5 Hans Dittmar

NATIONAL MEDAL COUNT

COMPETITORS   COUNTRIES: 44   ATHLETES: 3,092   MEN: 2,956   WOMEN: 136

	GOLD	SILVER	BRONZE	TOTAL		GOLD	SILVER	BRONZE	TOTAL		GOLD	SILVER	BRONZE	TOTAL		GOLD	SILVER	BRONZE	TOTAL
USA	45	27	27	99	BEL	3	7	3	13	ARG	1	3	2	6	URU	1	0	0	1
FRA	13	15	10	38	NOR	5	2	3	10	EST	1	1	4	6	ROM	0	0	1	1
FIN	14	13	10	37	NED	4	1	5	10	CAN	0	3	1	4	JPN	0	0	1	1
GBR	9	13	12	34	TCH	1	4	5	10	AUT	0	3	1	4	POR	0	0	1	1
SWE	4	13	12	29	DEN	2	5	2	9	RSA	1	1	1	3	HAI	0	0	1	1
SUI	7	8	10	25	HUN	2	3	4	9	YUG	2	0	0	2	NZL	0	0	1	1
ITA	8	3	5	16	AUS	3	1	2	6	POL	0	1	1	2					

MARCH 15 - APRIL 15

Art Competition
Architecture
Literature
Music
Painting
Sculpture

Sunday, MAY 4

PM	EVENT	VENUE
3:30	Rugby	Colombes stadium

Sunday, MAY 11

PM	EVENT	VENUE
3:30	Rugby	Colombes stadium

Sunday, MAY 18

PM	EVENT	VENUE
3:30	Rugby	Colombes stadium

Sunday, MAY 25

PM	EVENT	VENUE
3:30	Soccer	Colombes stadium . . . . Pershing Stadium . . . . preliminaries
5:15	Soccer	Pershing Stadium . . . . preliminaries
5:30	Soccer	Bergeyre Stadium . . . . preliminaries

Monday, MAY 26

PM	EVENT	VENUE
4:00	Soccer	Colombes stadium . . . . preliminaries
5:00	Soccer	Bergeyre Stadium . . . . preliminaries

Tuesday, MAY 27

PM	EVENT	VENUE
5:00	Soccer	Colombes stadium . . . . round of 16
6:00	Soccer	Paris Stadium . . . . round of 16

Wednesday, MAY 28

PM	EVENT	VENUE
5:00	Soccer	Colombes stadium . . . . round of 16
7:00	Soccer	Bergeyre Stadium . . . . round of 16

Thursday, MAY 29

PM	EVENT	VENUE
2:00	Soccer	Pershing Stadium . . . . round of 16
4:00	Soccer	Colombes stadium . . . . round of 16
5:00	Soccer	Bergeyre Stadium . . . . round of 16
5:00	Soccer	Paris Stadium . . . . round of 16

Sunday, JUNE 1

PM	EVENT	VENUE
4:00	Soccer	Colombes stadium . . . . quarterfinals
4:00	Soccer	Bergeyre Stadium . . . . quarterfinals

Monday, JUNE 2

PM	EVENT	VENUE
5:00	Soccer	Paris Stadium . . . . quarterfinals
5:00	Soccer	Bergeyre Stadium . . . . quarterfinals

Thursday, JUNE 5

PM	EVENT	VENUE
5:00	Soccer	Colombes stadium . . . . semifinals

Friday, JUNE 6

PM	EVENT	VENUE
5:00	Soccer	Colombes stadium . . . . semifinals

Sunday JUNE 8

PM	EVENT	VENUE
4:00	Soccer	Colombes stadium . . . . consolation (3 - 4 places, first of two games)

Monday, JUNE 9

PM	EVENT	VENUE
2:30	Soccer	Colombes stadium . . . . consolation (3 - 4 places, second game)
4:30	Soccer	Colombes stadium . . . . final

Monday, JUNE 23

AM	EVENT	VENUE
8:00	Shooting	Stand de la Sociètè de Tir de Reims . . . . 50-meter miniature rifles
PM	EVENT	VENUE
2:00	Shooting	Reims . . . . 50-meter miniature rifles

Thursday, JUNE 26

AM	EVENT	VENUE
8:00	Shooting	Champs des Chalon-Sur-Marne . . . . 400-meter free rifle, teams
PM	EVENT	VENUE
2:00	Shooting	Chalon-Sur-Marne . . . . 600-meter free rifle, teams

Friday, JUNE 27

AM	EVENT	VENUE
8:00	Shooting	Chalon-Sur-Marne . . . . 800-meter free rifle, teams

9:00	Fencing	Vélodrome d'Hiver . . . . team foil, preliminaries
PM	EVENT	
2:00	Fencing	Vélodrome d'Hiver . . . . team foil, preliminaries
2:00	Shooting	Chalon-Sur-Marne 600-meter free rifle, 3 positions

Saturday, JUNE 28

AM	EVENT	VENUE
9:00	Fencing	Vélodrome d'Hiver . . . . team foil, quarterfinals
PM	EVENT	
2:00	Fencing	Vélodrome d'Hiver . . . . team foil, quarterfinals
2:00	Shooting	Chalon-Sur-Marne . . . . 25-meter rapid-fire pistol
5:00	Polo	St. Cloud Country Club

Sunday, JUNE 29

AM	EVENT	VENUE
9:00	Fencing	Vélodrome d'Hiver . . . . team foil, semifinals
PM	EVENT	
2:00	Fencing	Vélodrome d'Hiver . . . . team foil, semifinals

Monday, JUNE 30

AM	EVENT	VENUE
9:00	Shooting	Versailles . . . . running deer (single shot)
9:00	Fencing	Vélodrome d'Hiver . . . . team foil, finals
PM	EVENT	VENUE
2:00	Fencing	Vélodrome d'Hiver . . . . team foil, finals

Tuesday, JULY 1

AM	EVENT	VENUE
9:00	Shooting	Versailles . . . . running deer (double shot)
9:00	Fencing	Vélodrome d'Hiver . . . . men's foil, preliminaries
PM	EVENT	VENUE
2:00	Fencing	Vélodrome d'Hiver . . . . men's foil, round of 16
5:00	Polo	St. Cloud Country Club

Wednesday, JULY 2

AM	EVENT	VENUE
9:00	Shooting	Versailles . . . . running deer (single shot), team
9:00	Fencing	Vélodrome d'Hiver . . . . women's individual foil, preliminaries
PM	EVENT	VENUE
2:00	Fencing	Vélodrome d'Hiver men's individual foil, quarterfinals
2:00	Shooting	Versailles . . . . running deer (single shot), team
5:00	Polo	Bagatelle (Bois de Boulogne)

Thursday, JULY 3

AM	EVENT	VENUE
9:00	Shooting	Versailles . . . . running deer (single shot), team
9:00	Fencing	Vélodrome d'Hiver women's individual foil, semifinals
PM	EVENT	VENUE
2:00	Fencing	Vélodrome d'Hiver men's individual foil, semifinals
2:00	Shooting	Versailles . . . . running deer (single shot), team
5:00	Polo	St. Cloud Country Club

Friday, JULY 4

AM	EVENT	VENUE
9:00	Fencing	Vélodrome d'Hiver . . women's individual foil, finals
PM	EVENT	VENUE
2:00	Fencing	Vélodrome d'Hiver . . . . men's individual foil, finals
5:00	Polo	St. Cloud Clountry Club
9:00	Fencing	Vélodrome d'Hiver . . . . men's individual foil, finals . . . . women's foil, finals

Saturday, JULY 5

PM	EVENT	VENUE
2:00	Opening Ceremony	Colombes stadium

Sunday, JULY 6

AM	EVENT	VENUE
9:00	Wrestling	Vélodrome d'Hiver . . Greco-Roman (all six weight classes), preliminaries
9:00	Shooting Stand Gastinne-Renette	Issy-les-Moulineaux . . . . clay target, individual
9:30	Fencing	Colombes Annex . . . . team épée, preliminaries
PM	EVENT	VENUE
2:00	Wrestling	Vélodrome d'Hiver Greco-Roman (all weight classes), preliminaries
2:00	Fencing	Colombes Annex . . . . team épée, preliminaries
3:00	Athletics	Colombes stadium . . . . men's 400-meter hurdles, 1st round; men's high jump, qualifications; men's javelin, qualifications & finals; (3:30) men's 100 meters, 1st round; (4:15) men's 800 meters, 1st round; (5:00) men's 100 meters, 2nd round; (5:30) men's 400-meter hurdles, 2nd round; (6:00) men's 10,000 meters, finals
5:00	Fencing	Colombes Annex . . . . team épée, preliminaries
6:00	Polo	St. Cloud Country Club

Monday, JULY 7

AM	EVENT	VENUE
9:00	Shooting	Plateau d'Issy . . . . clay targets, individual
9:00	Wrestling	Vélodrome d'Hiver . . Greco-Roman (all weights), preliminaries

9:00 Fencing ..... Colombes Annex ..... team épée, second round

PM	EVENT	VENUE
2:00	Shooting .... Plateau d'Issy ...... clay targets, individual	
2:00	Wrestling .. Vélodrome d'Hiver ... Greco-Roman (all weights), ... preliminaries	
2:00	Fencing ..... Colombes Annex ..... team épée, second round	
3:00	Athletics ... Colombes stadium .. men's 100 meters, semifinals; .. Pentathlon (long jump); (3:45) Pentathlon (javelin); (4:00) men's 400-meter hurdles, finals; men's high jump, finals;(4:30).. men's 800 meters, semifinals; (4:45) ... pentathlon (200 meters); (5:15) .. 3,000-meter steeplechase,...... preliminaries; (5:30) . pentathlon (discus); (6:00) men's 100 meters,. final; (6:15) pentathlon (1,500 meters)	
6:00	Polo ... St. Cloud Country Club	
9:00	Wrestling ... Vélodrome d'Hiver ... Greco-Roman (all weights), ... preliminaries	

Tuesday, JULY 8

AM	EVENT	VENUE
9:00	Shooting ... Issy-les Moulineaux ...... clay targets, individual	
9:00	Wrestling ... Vélodrome d'Hiver ... Greco-Roman (all weights), ... preliminaries	
9:00	Fencing ..... Colombes Annex ..... team épée, third round	

PM	EVENT
2:00	Fencing ..... Colombes Annex ..... team épée, third round
2:00	Shooting... Issy-les Moulineaux ...... clay targets, individual
2:00	Wrestling .. Vélodrome d'Hiver ... Greco-Roman (all weights), ... preliminaries
3:00	Athletics.... Colombes stadium ..... men's 110-meter hurdles, . preliminaries; men's long jump, qualifications & finals; (3:30).... men's 200 meters, first round; ... (4:00) men's shot put, eliminations & finals; (4:15) men's 800 meters, finals; .. (4:40) men's 110-meter . hurdles, semifinals; (5:00) men's 5,000 meter, preliminaries; (6:00). men's 200 meters, second round
9:00	Wrestling... Vélodrome d'Hiver ... Greco-Roman (all weights), ... preliminaries

Wednesday, JULY 9

AM	EVENT	VENUE
9:00	Shooting... Issy-les Moulineaux .... clay targets, team	
9:00	Fencing ..... Colombes Annex .... team épée, finals	
9:00	Wrestling .. Vélodrome d'Hiver ... Greco-Roman (all weights), ... quarterfinals	

PM	EVENT
2:00	Shooting... Issy-les Moulineaux .... clay targets, team
2:00	Fencing ..... Colombes Annex .... team épée, finals
2:00	Wrestling.. Vélodrome d'Hiver ... Greco-Roman (all weights), ... quarterfinals

3:00 Athletics.... Colombes stadium . men's 200 meters, semifinals;.... pole vault, qualifications; (3:30) . men's 110-meter hurdles, finals;.. (3:45) men's 10,000-meter walk, . preliminaries; men's 200 meters, . finals; (5:00) men's 1,500 meters,. preliminaries; (5:45) men's 3,000-meter steeplechase, finals; (6:00) . 10,000-meter walk, second round

5:00 Polo ... St. Cloud Country Club

Thursday, JULY 10

PM	EVENT	VENUE
9:00	Wrestling... Vélodrome d'Hiver Greco-Roman (all weights), finals	
9:00	Fencing ..... Colombes Annex .. individual épée, preliminaries	
2:00	Wrestling... Vélodrome d'Hiver Greco-Roman (all weights), finals	
2:00	Fencing ..... Colombes Annex .. individual épée, quarterfinals	
2:30	Yachting .... Meulan ...... monotype, first round .... (first & second runs)	
3:00	Athletics.... Colombes stadium . men's 400 meters, first round; ... hammer throw, qualifications and finals; pole vault, finals; men's 1,500 meters, finals; men's 5,000 meters,. finals; 400 meters, second round.	
5:00	Polo ... St. Cloud Country Club	
9:00	Wrestling... Vélodrome d'Hiver Greco-Roman (all weights), finals	

Friday , JULY 11

AM	EVENT	VENUE
9:00	Wrestling... Vélodrome d'Hiver freestyle (all seven weight classes), ... preliminaries	
9:00	Fencing ..... Colombes Annex .... individual épée, semifinals	

PM	EVENT
2:00	Fencing ..... Colombes Annex ...... individual épée, finals
2:00	Wrestling.. Vélodrome d'Hiver freestyle (all seven weight classes), ... preliminaries
2:30	Yachting .... Meulan ...... monotype, 2nd round .... (1st & 2nd runs)
3:00	Athletics.... Colombes stadium . decathlon (100 meters); (3:45) . men's 400 meters, semifinals;.... .. decathlon (long jump); (4:15) . ..... men's 3,000 meters, team . qualifications; (5:00) men's 10,000-meter walk, final; decathlon (shot. put); (5:45) decathlon (high jump); (6:30) men's 400 meters, finals; .. .. (6:45) decathlon (400 meters)
9:00	Wrestling... Vélodrome d'Hiver freestyle (all seven weight classes), ... preliminaries

Saturday, JULY 12

AM	EVENT	VENUE
9:00	Wrestling... Vélodrome d'Hiver freestyle (all weights), quarterfinals	
9:00	Fencing ..... Colombes Annex .... team saber, preliminaries	

PM	EVENT	VENUE
2:00	Wrestling... Vélodrome d'Hiver freestyle (all weights), quarterfinals	
2:00	Fencing ..... Colombes Annex ..... team saber, preliminaries	

2:00 Modern Pentathlon... Versailles .... shooting

2:30 Yachting .... Meulan ..... monotype, first semifinals

3:00 Athletics.... Colombes stadium . decathlon (110-meter hurdles);... triple jump, qualifications and ... finals; (3:30) 10,000-meter cross-. country, individual and team;.... decathlon (discus throw); (3:45) .. .... men's 4 x 100-meter relay, . preliminaries; (4:30) . decathlon . pole vault); (5:00) men's 4x400-.. meter relay, preliminaries and ... finals; (5:30) decathlon (javelin);.. (6:30) decathlon (1,500 meters), .. final event) ....

5:00 Polo ... St. Cloud Country Club

9:00 Wrestling... Vélodrome d'Hiver freestyle (all weights), quarterfinals

Sunday, JULY 13

AM	EVENT	VENUE
9:00	Wrestling... Vélodrome d'Hiver freestyle (all weights), semifinals	
9:00	Fencing ..... Colombes Annex ...... team saber, semifinals	
9:00	Tennis ..... Colombes Annex ... men's singles, preliminaries	
10:30	Swimming . Piscine de Tourelles ... men's 1,500-meter freestyle, ... preliminaries	
11:45	Water Polo......... Tourelles .... preliminaries	

PM	EVENT	VENUE
2:00	Fencing ..... Colombes Annex ...... team saber, semifinals	
2:00	Tennis ..... Colombes Annex ... men's singles, preliminaries; . women's singles, preliminaries	
2:00	Yachting........... Meulan .... monotype, semifinals	
2:30	Rowing.... Bassin D'Argenteuil . . pair-oared, preliminaries; four-. oared with coxswain, preliminar-. ies; plus canoeing demonstration	
3:30	Swimming .... Tourelles ... men's 1,500-meter freestyle, ... preliminaries; women's 400-. meter freestyle, preliminaries	
4:00	Athletics ... Colombes stadium men's 10,000-meter walk, finals; discus throw, qualification & finals; men's 4 x 100-meter relay, semifinals and finals; men's 3,000 meters, team, finals; marathon; men's 4 x 400-meter relay, finals	
4:30	Water Polo......... Tourelles .... preliminaries	
5:00	Water Polo......... Tourelles .... preliminaries	
9:00	Wrestling... Vélodrome d'Hiver freestyle (all weights), semifinals	

Monday, JULY 14

AM	EVENT	VENUE
9:00	Wrestling... Vélodrome d'Hiver ... freestyle (all weights), finals.	
9:00	Fencing ..... Colombes Annex ...... team saber, semifinals	
9:00	Tennis ..... Colombes Annex ... men's singles, preliminaries; . women's singles, preliminaries; ... men's doubles, preliminaries	
10:30	Swimming .... Tourelles ...... men's platform diving,	

.... qualifications

11:15 Water Polo........ Tourelles .... preliminaries

PM	EVENT	VENUE
2:00	Fencing ..... Colombes Annex ...... team saber, semifinals	
2:00	Tennis ..... Colombes Annex ... men's singles, preliminaries; . women's singles, preliminaries; .. men's doubles, preliminaries; women's doubles, preliminaries; .. mixed doubles, preliminaries	
2:00	Modern Pentathlon .. Tourelles .... swimming	
2:00	Rowing .... Argenteuil .... single sculls, preliminaries; ... pair-oared with coxswain, preliminaries; four-oared without ...... coxswain, preliminaries; .. plus canoeing demonstration	
3:00	Swimming ... men's 1,500-meter .. freestyle, semifinals; women's . 400-meter freestyle, semifinals	
4:30	Water Polo.... Tourelles .... preliminaries	
5:00	Water Polo .... Tourelles .... preliminaries	

Tuesday, JULY 15

AM	EVENT	VENUE
9:00	Fencing ..... Colombes Annex ...... team saber, finals	
9:00	Tennis ..... Colombes Annex ... men's singles, preliminaries; . women's singles, preliminaries; .. men's doubles, preliminaries; ... mixed doubles, round of 16	
9:00	Modern Pentathlon .... Colombes Annex .... fencing semifinal	
9:30	Swimming .... Tourelles .. men's 200-meter breaststroke, ... preliminaries	
10:30	Water Polo.... Tourelles .... quarterfinals	
11:15	Water Polo.... Tourelles .... quarterfinals	

PM	EVENT	VENUE
2:00	Rowing .... Argenteuil double sculls, preliminaries; eight-oared with coxswain, preliminaries; .. plus canoeing demonstration	
2:00	Fencing .... Colombes Annex .... team saber, finals	
2:00	Yachting........... Meulan .... monotype, finals	
2:00	Tennis ..... Colombes Annex men's singles, preliminaries and . round of 16; women's singles, . preliminaries and round of 16; men's doubles, preliminaries and . round of 16; women's doubles, . preliminaries and round of 16; .. mixed doubles, preliminaries	
2:00	Modern Pentathlon .... Colombes Annex Fencing............. finals	
2:30	Boxing .... Vélodrome d'Hiver .... preliminary bouts	
3:00	Swimming .... men's 1,500-meter freestyle, finals; women's 400 meters, finals	
4:15	Water Polo........ Tourelles .... quarterfinals	
5:00	Water Polo .... Tourelles .... quarterfinals	
9:00	Boxing .... Vélodrome d'Hiver .... preliminary bouts	

Wednesday, JULY 16

AM	EVENT	VENUE
9:00	Fencing . . . . . Colombes Annex . individual saber, preliminaries
9:00	Tennis . . . . . . Colombes Annex . . . . men's singles, round of 16; . women's singles, round of 16; men's doubles, preliminaries and . round of 16; women's doubles, . preliminaries and round of 16
10:30	Swimming . . . . Tourelles . . . . men's springboard diving, . qualifications; men's 100-meter . . . . . backstroke, preliminaries

PM	EVENT	VENUE
2:00	Fencing . . . . . Colombes Annex . individual saber, preliminaries
2:00	Rowing . . . . Argenteuil . . . . repechages
2:30	Boxing . . . . Vélodrome d'Hiver preliminary bouts and round of 16
3:00	Modern Pentathlon Fountainebleu . . . . riding
3:00	Swimming . . . . Tourelles women's 200-meter breaststroke, . preliminaries; men's 200-meter . breaststroke, semifinals; men's 400-meter freestyle, preliminaries
4:30	Water Polo . . . . Tourelles . . . . semifinals
5:00	Water Polo . . . . Tourelles . . . . semifinals
9:00	Boxing . . . . Vélodrome d'Hiver . . . . round of 16

Thursday JULY 17

AM	EVENT	VENUE
9:00	Fencing . . . . . Colombes Annex . . . . individual saber, semifinals
9:00	Gymnastics . Colombes stadium . . . . nine events
10:30	Swimming . . . . Tourelles . . women's springboard diving, . qualifications; men's 400-meter freestyle, semifinals; men's 100- . . . meter backstroke, semifinals

PM	EVENT	VENUE
2:00	Fencing . . . . Colombes Annex . . . . individual saber, semifinal
2:00	Rowing . . . . Argenteuil . single sculls, finals; pair-oared, ... finals; double skulls, finals; pair-oared with coxswain, finals; four-oared without coxswain; four-oared with coxswain; eight-oared . . . . finals
2:00	Boxing . . . . Vélodrome d'Hiver . . . . round of 16
2:00	Tennis . . . . . . Colombes Annex . . . men's singles, quarterfinals; . women's singles, quarterfinals; women's doubles, preliminaries; . . . mixed doubles, round of 16
3:00	Modern Pentathlon . . . . Colombes stadium . . . . running
3:00	Swimming . . . . Tourelles . men's springboard diving, finals; men's 200-meter breaststroke, finals
3:00	Gymnastics . Colombes stadium . . . . nine events
4:30	Water Polo . . . . Tourelles . . . . finals
8:00	Boxing . . . . Vélodrome d'Hiver . . . . round of 16

Friday, JULY 18

AM	EVENT	VENUE
9:00	Fencing . . . . . Colombes Annex . . . . individual saber, finals

9:00	Tennis . . . . . Colombes Annex . . . . men's singles, semifinals; . . . women's singles, semifinals; . . . men's doubles, quarterfinals
10:30	Swimming . . . . Tourelles women's 400-meter relays; men's . 800-meter relays, preliminaries

PM	EVENT	VENUE
1:30	Gymnastics (Jeux de Enfance) . . . . Colombes stadium . . . . demonstration
2:00	Boxing . . . . Vélodrome d'Hiver . . . . quarterfinals
2:00	Fencing . . . . Colombes Annex . . . . individual saber, finals
3:00	Swimming . . . . Tourelles men's 400-meter freestyle, finals; . . women's springboard diving, . . finals; men's 800-meter relay, . . semifinals; men's 100-meter backstroke, finals; women's 200- . . . . . . meter breaststroke, finals
3:00	Gymnastics . Colombes stadium . . . . nine events
9:00	Boxing . . . . Vélodrome d'Hiver . . . . quarterfinals

Saturday, JULY 19

AM	EVENT	VENUE
9:00	Gymnastics . Colombes stadium . . . . nine events
9:00	Tennis . . . . . Colombes Annex . . . . men's doubles, semifinals; women's doubles, finals; mixed . . . . doubles, quarterfinals
10:00	Swimming . . . . Tourelles men's 100-meter freestyle, finals; men's platform diving, preliminaries

PM	EVENT	VENUE
2:00	Gymnastics (Jeux de Enfance) . . . . Colombes stadium . . . . demonstration
2:00	Swimming . . . . Tourelles . . . men's 100-meter freestyle, . . semifinals; women's platform . diving, qualifications; women's 100-meter backstroke, qualifications
2:00	French Boxing Vélodrome d'Hiver . . . . demonstration sport
2:00	Gymnastics . Colombes stadium . . . . nine events
8:00	Boxing . . . . Vélodrome . . . . semifinals

Sunday, JULY 20

AM	EVENT	VENUE
10:00	Swimming . . . . Tourelles women's 100-meter freestyle, semifinals; men's 800-meter relay, finals

PM	EVENT	VENUE
2:00	Tennis . . . . . . Colombes Annex . . men's singles, finals; women's . . singles, finals; mixed doubles,

	. . . . semifinals
2:00	Gymnastics . Colombes stadium . . . . nine events
2:00	Gymnastics (Jeux de Enfance) . . . . Colombes stadium . . . . demonstration
2:00	Swimming . . . . Tourelles . . men's platform diving, finals; women's platform diving, finals;
	men's 100-meter freestyle, finals; . . women's 100-meter freestyle, ... finals; women's 100-meter . . . . backstroke, finals
8:00	Boxing . . . . Vélodrome d'Hiver . . . . finals

Monday, JULY 21

PM	EVENT	VENUE
2:00	Equestrian Sports . . . . Colombes stadium . . . dressage (individual & team)
2:00	Tennis . . . . . Colombes Annex . . . . men's doubles, finals; . . . . mixed doubles, finals
2:00	Weight lifting Vélodrome d'Hiver . . . featherweight, preliminaries
2:00	Yachting . . . . Le Havre . . . . 8 meter, first race; . . . . 6 meter, first race
5:00	Pelote Basque . . Fronton de Paris . . . . demonstration sport
9:00	Weight lifting . Vélodrome d'Hiver . . . . featherweight, finals

Tuesday, JULY 22

AM	EVENT	VENUE
9:00	Weight lifting Vélodrome d'Hiver . . . . lightweight, preliminaries

PM	EVENT	VENUE
2:00	Equestrian Sports . . . . Colombes stadium . . . dressage (individual & team)
2:00	Weight lifting Vélodrome d'Hiver . . . . lightweight, finals
2:00	Yachting . . . . Le Havre . . . . 8-meter, second race; . . . . 6-meter, second race
5:00	Pelote Basque . . Fronton de Paris . . . . demonstration sport
8:00	Weight lifting . Vélodrome d'Hiver . . . . middleweight preliminaries

Wednesday, JULY 23

AM	EVENT	VENUE
8:00	Cycling . . . . Colombes stadium . . . . 188-kilometer road race, . . individual and team time trial
9:00	Weight lifting Vélodrome d'Hiver . . . . middleweight, finals; light . . . heavyweight, preliminaries

	. . . . semifinals
2:00	Gymnastics . Colombes stadium . . . . nine events
2:00	Gymnastics (Jeux de Enfance) . . . . Colombes stadium . . . . demonstration
2:00	Swimming . . . . Tourelles . . men's platform diving, finals; women's platform diving, finals;
8:00	Boxing . . . . Vélodrome d'Hiver . . . . finals

PM	EVENT	VENUE
2:00	Yachting . . . . Le Havre . . . . 8-meter, third race; . . . . 6-meter, third race
5:00	Pelote Basque . . Fronton de Paris . . . . demonstration sport
8:00	Weight lifting Vélodrome d'Hiver light heavyweight, preliminaries

Thursday, JULY 24

AM	EVENT	VENUE
5:00	Equestrian Sports . . Hippodrome . . . . d'Auteuil endurance (individual and team)

PM	EVENT	VENUE
2:00	Yachting . . . . Le Havre . . . . 8-meter, fourth race; . . . . 6-meter, fourth race
2:00	Weight lifting Vélodrome d'Hiver super heavyweight, preliminaries
5:00	Pelote Basque . . Fronton de Paris . . . . demonstration sport
8:00	Weight lifting Vélodrome d'Hiver . . . . super heavyweight, finals

Friday, JULY 25

AM	EVENT	VENUE
5:00	Equestrian Sports . . . . Colombes stadium . . . . dressage (individual)

PM	EVENT	VENUE
2:00	Yachting . . . . Le Havre . . . . 8-meter, first semifinal; . . . . 6-meter, first semifinal
3:00	Equestrian Sports . . . . Colombes stadium . . . . dressage (individual)

Saturday, JULY 26

PM	EVENT	VENUE
2:00	Yachting . . . . Le Havre . . . 8-meter, second semifinal; . . . . 6-meter, second semifinal
2:30	Cycling . . . . Piste de Vincennes . . . . men's 1,000-meter sprint, preliminaries; men's 2,000-meter . . tandem, preliminaries; men's . . . 4,000-meter team pursuit, preliminaries; men's 4,000-meter . . . . team pursuit, quarterfinals
3:00	Equestrian Sports . . . . Colombes stadium . . . . show jumping . . . . (individual and team)

Sunday, JULY 27

PM	EVENT	VENUE
2:30	Cycling . . . . Piste de Vincennes . . . . . men's 1,000-meter sprint, quarterfinals; men's 1,000-meter . . . sprint, semifinals; men's 50- . . . kilometer track race; men's . . . 2,000-meter tandem, finals; men's 4,000-meter team pursuit, semifinals; men's 4,000-meter team . pursuit, finals; men's 1,000-meter . . . . sprint, finals
3:00	Equestrian Sports . . . . Colombes stadium show jumping (individual & team)

FOLLOWING JUMPING FINALS
Closing Ceremony . . . . Colombes stadium

ST. MORITZ 1928
2ND OLYMPIC WINTER GAMES

BOBSLED

FOUR-MAN	USA 3:20.5	USA 3:21.0	GER 3:21.9

FIGURE SKATING

SINGLES	SWE 12 1,630.75 GILLIS GRAFSTRÖM	AUT 13 1,625.50 WILLY BÖCKL	BEL 27 1,542.75 ROBERT VAN ZEEBROECK
SINGLES	NOR 8 2,452.25 SONJA HENIE	AUT 25 2,248.50 FRITZI BURGER	USA 28 2,254.50 BEATRIX LOUGHRAN
PAIRS	FRA 14 100.50 ANDRÉE JOLY PIERRE BRUNET	AUT 17 99.25 LILLI SCHOLZ OTTO KAISER	AUT 29 93.25 MELITTA BRUNNER LUDWIG WREDE

ICE HOCKEY

FINAL STANDINGS	CAN	SWE	SUI

SKELETON

SINGLE	USA 3:01.8 JENNISON HEATON	USA 3:02.8 JOHN HEATON	GBR 3:05.1 DAVID, EARL OF NORTHESK

NORDIC SKIING

15/18 KM CROSS-COUNTRY 19.7 KM	NOR 1:37:01.0 JOHAN GRÖTTUMSBRATEN	NOR 1:39:01.0 OLE HEGGE	NOR 1:40:11.0 REIDAR ÖDEGAARD
50-KM CROSS-COUNTRY, CLASSICAL	SWE 4:52:03.0 PER ERIK HEDLUND	SWE 5:05:30.0 GUSTAF JONSSON	SWE 5:05:46.0 VOLGER ANDERSSON

SKI JUMPING

LARGE HILL	NOR 19.208 ALF ANDERSEN	NOR 18.542 SIGMUND RUUD	TCH 17.937 RUDOLF BURKERT

NORDIC COMBINED

INDIVIDUAL	NOR 17.833 JOHAN GRÖTTUMSBRATEN	NOR 15.303 HANS VINJARENGEN	NOR 15.021 JOHN SNERSRUD

SPEED SKATING

500 METER	**FIN** 43.4 *CLAS THUNBERG*		**USA** 43.6 *JOHN FARRELL*
	NOR 43.4 *BERNT EVENSEN*		**NOR** 43.6 *ROALD LARSEN*
			FIN 43.6 *JAAKKO FRIMAN*
1,500 METER	**FIN** 2:21.1 *CLAS THUNBERG*	**NOR** 2:21.9 *BERNT EVENSEN*	**NOR** 2:22.6 *IVAR BALLANGRUD*
5,000 METER	**NOR** 8:50.5 *IVAR BALLANGRUD*	**FIN** 8:59.1 *JULIUS SKUTNABB*	**NOR** 9:01.1 *BERNT EVENSEN*

* Men's 10,000 meter event cancelled

NATIONAL MEDAL COUNT

COMPETITORS   COUNTRIES: 25   ATHLETES: 464   MEN: 438   WOMEN: 26

	GOLD	SILVER	BRONZE	TOTAL		GOLD	SILVER	BRONZE	TOTAL		GOLD	SILVER	BRONZE	TOTAL		GOLD	SILVER	BRONZE	TOTAL
NOR	6	4	5	15	FIN	2	1	1	4	CAN	1	0	0	1	BEL	0	0	1	1
USA	2	2	2	6	AUT	0	3	1	4	GER	0	0	1	1	TCH	0	0	1	1
SWE	2	2	1	5	FRA	1	0	0	1	SUI	0	0	1	1	GBR	0	0	1	1

ST. MORITZ 1928 PROGRAM OF EVENTS

Saturday, FEBRUARY 11

AM	EVENT	VENUE
10:00	Opening Ceremony . . . . Olympic Stadium	
FOLLOWING THE CEREMONIES . . . . Hockey Four Games		

Sunday, FEBRUARY 12

AM	EVENT	VENUE
8:00	Military Skiing . . . . Chantarella to Salet . . . . team race, demonstration sport	
8:30	Hockey . . . . Olympic Stadium	
10:00	Hockey . . . . Olympic Stadium	
11:30	Hockey . . . . Olympic Stadium	

PM	EVENT	VENUE
1:00	Hockey . . . . Olympic Stadium	
AFTERNOON Horseracing on Snow . . . . Lake St. Moritz galloping (2 races); steeplechase (1 race); trotting (1 race); Skijöring (2 races); demonstration sport		

Monday, FEBRUARY 13

AM	EVENT	VENUE
8:00	Speed Skating . . . . Olympic Stadium . . . . 500 meters	
10:00	Hockey	

PM	EVENT	VENUE
1:00	Speed Skating . . . . Olympic Stadium . . . . 5,000 meters	

Tuesday, FEBRUARY 14

AM	EVENT	VENUE
8:00	Cross-Country Skiing . . . . Salet . . . . 50 kilometers	

8:30	Speed Skating . . . . Olympic Stadium . . . . 1,500 meters	
9:00	Figure Skating . . . . Kulm Ice Rink . . . . men's set figures	
NOON	Speed Skating . . . . Olympic Stadium . . . . 10,000 meters	

Wednesday, FEBRUARY 15

Events canceled due to weather

Thursday, FEBRUARY 16

AM	EVENT	VENUE
9:00	Hockey . . . . Olympic Stadium	
10:30	Hockey . . . . Olympic Stadium	

PM	EVENT	VENUE
1:30	Hockey . . . . Olympic Stadium	
2:00	Figure Skating . . . . Kulm Ice Rink . . . . women's figures	
3:00	Hockey . . . . Olympic Stadium . . . . Final round	

Friday, FEBRUARY 17

AM	EVENT	VENUE
8:00	Cross-Country Skiing . . . . Salet . . . . 18 kilometer	
8:00	Skeleton . . . . Cresta Run	
8:30	Hockey . . . . Olympic Stadium . . . . Final round	
9:00	Figure Skating . . . . Kulm Ice Rink . . . . men's freestyle	
10:00	Hockey . . . . Olympic Stadium . . . . Final round	

PM	EVENT	VENUE
2:00	Figure Skating . . . . Kulm Ice Rink . . . . women's freestyle	

Saturday, FEBRUARY 18

AM	EVENT	VENUE
8:00	Bobsled . . . . St. Moritz Bobbahn	
8:30	Hockey . . . . Olympic Stadium . . . . Final round	
8:30	Figure Skating . . . . Kulm Ice Rink . . . . women's freestyle	
10:00	Cross-Country Skiing . . . . Salet and St. . . . . Moritz Olympic Ski Jump . . . . Combined event	
10:00	Hockey . . . . Olympic Stadium . . . . Final round	

PM	EVENT	VENUE
2:00	Ski Jumping . . . . St. Moritz Olympic . . . . Ski Jump . . . . Regular Hill	

Sunday, FEBRUARY 19

AM	EVENT	VENUE
9:00	Figure Skating . . . . Kulm Ice Rink . . . . Pairs	
9:15	Hockey . . . . Olympic Stadium . . . . Final round	

PM	EVENT	VENUE
1:30	Hockey . . . . Olympic Stadium . . . . Final round	
FOLLOWING THE GAME. . . . . Closing Ceremony . . . . Olympic Stadium		

RECORD OF THE VIII OLYMPIAD

MAY 4, 1924–MAY 16, 1928

OFFICERS OF THE INTERNATIONAL OLYMPIC COMMITTEE

Baron Pierre de Coubertin   President
Godefroy de Blonay   Vice President

Other Executive Members:
Count Henri de Baillet-Latour (Elected third IOC president on May 28, 1925)
J. Sigfrid Edström
Jiri Guth-Jarkovsky
Marquis Melchoir de Polignac

INTERNATIONAL OLYMPIC COMMITTEE MEMBERSHIP DURING THE VIII OLYMPIAD

ARRIVALS: 19

—— 1924 ——

June 25	Peter Scharroo	Netherlands
	Seiichi Kishi	Japan
July 9	Jorge Gomez de Parada	Mexico
November 7	Theodor Lewald*	Germany
	Oscar Ruperti*	Germany
	James Taylor*	Australia
	Martin Haudek*	Austria
	Duke of Alba*	Spain
	Khan Samad*	Persia

—— 1925 ——

January 18	David Kinley*	United States
May 26	Shimmelpenninck van der Oye	Netherlands
May 26	Alberto Bonavossa	Italy
October 2	Joseph Firth*	New Zealand

—— 1926 ——

March 24	Georges Averov*	Greece
	Thomas Fearnley	Norway
May 5	Adolf von Mecklenburg	Germany
	Janis Dikmanis	Latvia
April 22	Lord Rochdale	Great Britain
	Ernest Lee Jahncke	United States

* Elected by postal vote.

DEPARTURES: 11

—— 1924 ——

July 9	Carlos de Guadeloupe	Mexico

—— 1925 ——

May 26	Alexandre Mercati	Greece
May 28	Baron Pierre de Coubertin	France
May 28	William Milligan Sloane	United States
October	Arthur Marryatt	New Zealand

—— 1927 ——

January 16	Robert de Courcy-Laffan*	Great Britain
April 13	Jorge Gomez de Parada	Mexico
April 22	Johan Sverre	Norway
April 24	Khan Samad	Persia
	David Kinley	United States
	Duke of Alba	Spain

*Died in office; all others resigned.

Net increase in the IOC membership: 8

Total IOC membership by the end of the VIII Olympiad: 66

OFFICERS OF THE UNITED STATES OLYMPIC COMMITTEE

On November 22, 1922, the USOC, then known as the American Olympic Association (AOA), adopted its first constitution, which called for a quadrennial meeting to elect officers to four-year terms. The new constitution also mandated the creation of a second, temporary organization to be known as the American Olympic Committee, or AOC. Junior to the permanent AOA, the AOC was to become active a year before each Games to raise money for fielding an American team. The AOC was also to have its own president. The two-committee structure was destined to cause the AOA problems.

1st U.S. quadrennial, November 22, 1922–November 17, 1926

Colonel Robert M. Thompson
Thompson, who had also served two terms as president prior the new constitution, was concurrently elected president of the AOA and the AOC.

Other elected officers were:
Maj. Gen. Henry T. Allen, Vice President/Executive Officer
Henry G. Lapham, First Vice President
Dwight F. Davis, Second Vice President
William F. Humphrey, Third Vice President
Frederick W. Rubien, Secretary
Julius H. Barnes, Treasurer
John T. McGovern, Councillor

2nd U.S. quadrennial, November 17, 1926–November 19, 1930

William C. Prout
Prout was concurrently elected president of the AOA and the AOC, although he had separate vice presidents for each organization. His death on August 28, 1927, led to a constitutional crisis within the American Olympic establishment.

Other elected officers were:
Maj. Gen. Henry T. Allen, Vice President/Executive Officer
Dr. Graeme H. Hammond, First Vice President
Dwight F. Davis, Second Vice President
William F. Humphrey, Third Vice President
Frederick W. Rubien, Secretary
Julius H. Barnes, Treasurer
John T. McGovern, Councillor

Dr. Graeme H. Hammond
The first vice president of the AOA, Hammond automatically assumed the presidency on August 28, 1927, and served to the end of the quadrennial term. However, the three vice presidents of the AOC refused to acknowledge his leadership of the lesser organization. As a compromise, Major General Douglas MacArthur was elected first vice president of the AOC, and he succeeded to the AOC presidency on September 27, 1927. MacArthur's mandate was to organize and see to the funding of the American team for the Amsterdam 1928 Games. MacArthur's election has resulted in the frequent misapprehension that he once served as a USOC president. He did not; Dr. Hammond held that office throughout the second U.S. quadrennial.

HONORARY PRESIDENTS OF THE UNITED STATES OLYMPIC COMMITTEE

Starting with President Grover Cleveland, who accepted the honorary presidency of what was then the American Olympic Committee in December, 1895, every United States president has agreed to serve in this capacity. During the VIII Olympiad, President Calvin Coolidge was the honorary president of the AOA.

OLYMPIC AWARDS

THE OLYMPIC CUP

Beginning in 1906, the Olympic Cup was awarded annually to a person, institution, or association that had contributed significantly to sport or to the development of the Olympic movement. The Olympic Cup was kept at the IOC; honorees received a reproduction. The award was originally conceived by Pierre de Coubertin.

RECIPIENTS

National Physical Education Committee of Uruguay, awarded July 8, 1924, for the year 1925
Norwegian Ski Federation, awarded May 28, 1925, for the year 1926
Colonel Robert M. Thompson, awarded May 6, 1926, for the year 1927
Mexico National Sporting Association, awarded April 23, 1927, for the year 1928

THE OLYMPIC DIPLOMA OF MERIT

The Olympic Diploma of Merit, created in 1905 during the III Olympic Congress at Brussels, was awarded to an individual who had been active in the service of sport or had contributed substantially to the Olympic movement.

RECIPIENTS

None

OFFICIAL PUBLICATIONS OF THE INTERNATIONAL OLYMPIC COMMITTEE

OLYMPIC CHARTER

The Olympic Charter provides the official rules, procedures, and protocols of the IOC, which are periodically updated by vote of the membership at an IOC session. Two editions were issued during the VIII Olympiad: Edition 6 in May, 1924, and Edition 6.1 in November, 1924. Both were published in French only.

OLYMPIC REVIEW AND INTERNATIONAL OLYMPIC COMMITTEE OFFICIAL BULLETIN (BULLETIN OFFICIEL DU COMITÉ INTERNATIONAL DES JEUX OLYMPIQUES)

Broke, demoralized, and unable to raise support within the IOC for publications, Pierre de Coubertin published no version of the *Olympic Review* or *Olympic Bulletin* for the nine remaining years of his presidency. All previous editions had been published and distributed at his expense. Shortly after Coubertin left office, the new president, Count Henri de Baillet-Latour, started the *Olympic Bulletin*, which created the seventh version of the *Olympic Review*, with its own numbering system. The new version was printed in French, German, Spanish, and English.

#1	January 1926
#2	April 1926
#3	July 1926
#4	October 1926
#5	January 1927
#6	March 1927
#7	June 1927
#8	September 1927
#9	December 1927
#10	April 1928

ACKNOWLEDGMENTS

The publisher would like to thank the following for their invaluable assistance to 1st Century Project and World Sport Research & Publications: Gov. Francisco G. Almeda (Philippine Olympic Committee, Manila); Sheik Fahad Al-Ahmad Al-Sabah (Olympic Committee of Kuwait); Don Anthony; Maj. Gen. Charouck Arirachakaran (Olympic Committee of Thailand, Bangkok); Bibliothèque National de France (Paris); Marie-Charlotte Bolot (University of the Sorbonne Cultural Library and Archives, Paris); Boston Public Library; British Museum and Library (London); Gail Britton; Richard L. Coe; Anita DeFrantz (IOC Member in the United States); Margi Denton; Carl and Lieselott Diem - Archives/Olympic Research Institute of the German Sport University Cologne; Edward L. Doheny, Jr. Library (University of Southern California, Los Angeles); Robert G. Engel; Miguel Fuentes (Olympic Committee of Chile, Santiago); National Library of Greece (Athens); Hollee Hazwell (Columbiana Collection, Columbia University, New York); Rebecca S. Jabbour and Bill Roberts (Bancroft Library, University of California at Berkeley); Diane Kaplan (Manuscripts and Archives, Sterling Library, Yale University, New Haven); David Kelly (Sport Specialist, Library of Congress, Washington, D.C.); Fékrou Kidane (International Olympic Committee, Lausanne); Peter Knight; Dr. John A. Lucas; Los Angeles Public Library; Blaine Marshall; Joachaim Mester, President of the German Sport University Cologne; Ed Mosk; Geoffroy de Navacelle; New York Public Library; Olympic Committee of India (New Delhi); Richard Palmer (British Olympic Association, London); C. Robert Paul; University of Rome Library and Archives; Margaret M. Sherry (Rare Books and Special Collections, Firestone Library, Princeton University); Dr. Ruth Sparhawk; Gisela Terrell (Special Collections, Irwin Library, Butler University, Indianapolis); The Officers, Directors and Staff (United States Olympic Committee, Colorado Springs); University Research Library, (University of California at Los Angeles); John Vernon (National Archives, Washington, DC); Emily C. Walhout (Houghton Library; Harvard University); Herb Weinberg; Dr. Wayne Wilson, Michael Salmon, Shirley Ito (Paul Ziffren Sports Resource Center Library, Amateur Athletic Foundation of Los Angeles); Patricia Henry Yeomans; Nanci A. Young (Seeley G. Mudd Manuscript Library, Princeton University Archives); David Wallechinsky; Dr. Karel Wendl, Michéle Veillard, Patricia Eckert, Simon Mandl, Ruth Perrenoud, Nikolay Guerguiev, Fani Kakridi-Enz , Laura Leslie Pearman, and Christine Sklentzas (International Olympic Committee Olympic Studies and Research Center, Lausanne); and Pat White (Special Collections, Stanford University Library, Palo Alto).

The publishers recognize with gratitude the special contributions made for Volume 8 by David Chapman; Catherine Fasel Chapuis, Alexandra Leclef Mandl (International Olympic Committee Photo Archives, Lausanne); Beth Davis (Figure Skating Hall of Fame, Colorado Springs); Linda Lemonds Fray; Deborah Goodsite (The Bettman Archive, New York); Kate Griffin; The Margaret Herrick Library of the Academy of Motion Pictures Arts and Sciences (Los Angeles); Pekka Honkanen, Jouni Heino, Juha Kanerva, Kaisa Laitinen (Finland Sports Museum and Library, Helsinki); Corina Huber (St. Moritz Historical Library); Preston Levi (International Swimming Hall of Fame, Ft. Lauderdale); Shigeaki Matsubara; Takamichi Mikami (Prince Chichibu Memorial Sports Museum, Tokyo); Yo Nagaya; Patricia Olkiewicz, Cindy Slater (United States Olympic Committee Library and Photo Archives, Colorado Springs); Aileen Riggin Soule; Jean-François Pitet; Gladys Serafino (Canadian Olympic Hall of Fame, Calgary); Manica Sketa (Olympic Committee of Slovenia, Ljubljana); and Jahn A. van Zuijlen, Marjet Derks (Netherlands Sports Museum, Lelystad).

The Publishers would also like to thank the following individuals, institutions and foundations for providing initial funding for the project: The Amelior Foundation (Morristown, New Jersey); Roy and Mary Cullen (Houston); The English, Bonter, Mitchell Foundation (Ft. Wayne, Indiana); Adrian French (Los Angeles); The Knight Foundation (Miami); The Levy Foundation (Philadelphia); and, Jonah Shacknai (New York). And for completion funding: Michael McKie, Optimax Securities, Inc. (Toronto); Graham Turner, Fraser & Beatty (Toronto); and Century of Sport Partnership (Toronto).

And a special thanks to Barron Pittenger (Assistant Executive Director, United States Olympic Committee, September 1981 to August 1987 and Executive Director, August 1987 to December 1989).

BIBLIOGRAPHY

Adelbert, Jacques. *La Vie Quotidienne en France, des Origines a nos Jours*. Paris: Larousse, 1989.

Albertson, Lisa H. (ed.). *Athens to Atlanta: 100 Years of Glory*. Salt Lake City, Utah: Mikko Laitinen Commemorative Publications, 1993.

Albertson, Lisa H. (ed.). *Chamonix to Lillehammer: The Glory of the Olympic Winter Games*. Salt Lake City, Utah: Mikko Laitinen Commemorative Publications, 1994.

The Amateur Fencing Association. *Know the Game: Fencing*. London: A & C Black, Ltd., 1994.

Arthur, Daley. *The Story of the Olympic Games*. New York: J.B. Lippincott Co., 1965.

Associated Press & Grolier. *Pursuit of Excellence: The Olympic Story*. Connecticut: Grolier Enterprises Inc., 1979.

Baillie, Kate and Tim Salmon. *Paris: The Rough Guide*. London: Rough Guides, Ltd., 1995.

Barzini, Luigi. *The Italians*. London: Penguin Books. Ltd., 1968.

Benyo, Richard. *The Masters of the Marathon*. New York: Atheneum, 1983.

Bö, Olav, (trans. by W. Edson Richmond). *Skiing Throughout History*. Oslo: Det Norske Samlaget, 1993.

Bolgy, Dr. Maurice. "The Olympic Games Today and Yesterday." *The Living Age*. May 17, 1924.

Burch, Lonnie and Louie Robinson. *The Black Olympians: 1904 - 1984*. Los Angeles: California Afro-American Museum, 1984.

Carlson, Lewis H. and John J. Fogarty. *Tales of Gold*. Chicago: Contemporary Books Inc., 1987.

Cowley, Malcom. *And I Worked at the Writer's Trade: Chapters of Literary History, 1918-1978*. New York: Penguin Books, 1978.

Cronin, Vincent. *Paris, City of Light, 1919-1939*. London: HarperCollins, 1995.

Crossman, Col. Jim. *Olympic Shooting*. Washington DC: National Rifle Association, 1978.

Culbertson, Judi and Tom Randall. *Permanent Parisians: An Illustrated Guide to the Cemeteries of Paris*. Chelsea, Vermont: Chelsea Green Publishing Company, 1986.

Dawson, Buck. *Weissmuller to Spitz...An Era to Remember*. Ft. Lauderdale, FL: International Swimming Hall of Fame, 1988.

Duncanson, Neil & Patrick Collins. *Tales of Gold*. London: Queen Anne Press, 1992.

Duncanson, Neil. *The Fastest Men on Earth*. London: Willow Books, 1988.

Dodd, Christopher. *The Story of World Rowing*. London: Stanley Paul.

Falls, Joe. *The Boston Marathon*. New York: Macmillan Publishing, 1977.

Gafner, Raymond (supervisor). *The International Olympic Committee-One Hundred Years: The Idea-The Presidents-The Achievements, Vol. I*. Lausanne: International Olympic Committee, 1994.

Gallico, Paul. *Farewell to Sport*. London: Simon & Schuster, Ltd., 1988.

Gaudreau, Leo. *Anvils, Horseshoes and Cannons: The History of Strongmen*. Self-Published, 1975.

Gordon, Barclay. *Olympic Architecture: Building for the Summer Games*. New York: John Wiley & Sons, 1983.

Gordon, Harry. *Australia and the Olympic Games*. St. Lucia, Queensland: University of Queensland Press, 1994.

Grombach, John V. *The 1968 Olympic Guide*. New York: Pyramid Books, 1968.

Guttman, Allen. *From Ritual to Record: The Nature of Modern Sports*. New York: Colombia University Press, 1978.

Guttman, Allen. *The Olympics: A History of the Modern Games*. Chicago and Urbana: University of Illinois Press, 1992.

Hannus, Matti. *Flying Finns: The Story of the Great Tradition of Finnish Distance Running and Cross-Country Skiing*. Helsinki: Tietosanoma Oy, 1990.

Henie, Sonja. *Wings On My Feet*. New York: Prentice-Hall Inc., 1940.

Henry, Bill. *An Approved History of the Olympic Games*. Los Angeles: The Southern California Committee for the Olympic Games, 1981.

Hemingway, Ernest A. *A Movable Feast*. New York: Charles Scribner's Sons, 1964.

Hugman, Barry J. and Peter Arnold. *The Olympic Games: Complete Track and Field Results*. New York: Facts on File, 1988.

Johnson, Douglas and Madeleine. *The Age of Illusion: Art and Politics in France, 1918-1940*. London: Thames and Hudson, 1987.

Kieran, John and Arthur Daley. *The Story of the Olympic Games*. New York: J.B. Lippincott Company, 1965.

Killanin, The Lord and John Rodda. *The Olympic Games 80 Years of People, Events and Records*. New York: Collier Books.

The Lawn Tennis Association Trust. *Know the Game: Tennis*. London: A & C Black, Ltd., 1994.

Leigh, Mary H. *The Evolution of Women's Participation in the Summer Olympic Games, 1900-1948*. Dissertation, The Ohio State University, 1974.

Lester, Gary. *Australians at the Olympics*. Sydney: Lester-Townsend Publishing PTY LTD., 1984.

Liebling, A. J. *The Sweet Science*. London: Penguin Books, 1983.

Lucas, John. *The Modern Olympic Games*. New York: A.S. Barnes and Co., 1980.

Magnusson, Sally. *The Flying Scotsman*. New York: Quarter Books, 1981.

Meuret, Jean-Louis. *The FISA Centenary Book*. Neuchatel, Switzerland: The International Rowing Federation, n.d.

Müller, Norbert. *One Hundred Years of Olympic Congresses, 1894-1994*. Paris: Special Edition for the Participants in the Centennial Olympic Congress, 1994.

Nason, Jerry. "King of Heartbreak Hill." *The Runner*, May 1979.

O'Neil, John. "The American Olympic Rugby Championship." *The Athletic Journal*, 1924.

Mellow, James R. *Hemingway: A Life Without Consequences*. London: Hodder & Stoughton, 1994.

Metropolitan Weather Office. *General Weather Reports International Section July 1924*. Bracknell: The Metropolitan Weather Office, 1994.

Phelps, Robert (trans.). *Letters from Colette*. New York: Farrar, Straus & Giroux, 1980.

Roxborough, Henry. *Canada At the Olympics*. Toronto: The Ryerson Press, 1963.

Sarde, Michele. *Colette: Free and Fettered*. New York: William Morrow and Co., 1980.

Schaap, Richard. *An Illustrated History of the Olympics*. New York: Alfred A. Knopf, 1963.

Smith, Bonnie G. *Confessions of a Concierge: Madame Lucie's History of Twentieth Century France*. New Haven and London: Yale University Press, 1985.

"Sports and Athletics." *The Literary Digest*, July 12, 1924.

"Sport and Athletics." *The Literary Digest*, June 21, 1922.

Seth-Smith, Michael. *The Cresta Run: History of the St. Moritz Tobogganing Club*. London: Foulsham, 1976.

Seville, Samuel Jr. "The Cleanlies." *The Independent*, Vol. 113.

Stein, Gertrude. *The Autobiography of Alice B. Toklas*. New York: Vintage Books, 1960.

Strait, Raymond and Leif Henie. *Queen of Ice Queen, of Shadows: The Unsuspected Life of Sonja Henie*. New York: Stein and Day, 1985.

The editors at Time-Life Books. *The World in Arms, AD 1900-1925*. Alexandria, VA: Time Life Books, 1990.

Taylor, A.J.P. *The Origins of the Second World War*. London: Hamish Hamilton, 1961.

Taylor-Wilkie, Doreen (ed.). *Insight Guides: Finland*. Hong-Kong: APA Publications (HK) Ltd., 1992.

Thompson, Robert M. *Report on VIII Olympiad: Paris, France, 1924*. American Olympic Association, 1924.

Tomkins, Calvin. *Living Well is the Best Revenge*. New York: The Viking Press, 1962.

Wallechinsky, David. *The Complete Book of the Olympics*. Boston: Little, Brown & Company, 1991.

Weyand, Alexander M. *The Olympic Pageant*. New York: The Macmillan Company, 1952.

Wilkie, David, and Kelvin Juba. *The Handbook of Swimming*. London: Penguin Books Ltd., 1990.

Wright, Benjamin T. *Skating Around the World, 1892-1992*. Davos, Switzerland: International Skating Union, 1992.

Zarnowski, Frank. *The Decathlon: A Colorful History of Track and Field's Most Challenging Event*. Chicago: Leisure Press, 1989.

1924 Excerpts from:

the *New York Times*

the *Times* of London

the *Los Angeles Times*

PHOTO CREDITS

THE OLYMPIC WORLD
1928 Winter Games

PARTICIPATING COUNTRIES

NORTH AMERICA

CAN..................................CANADA
MEX..................................MEXICO
USA..........UNITED STATES OF AMERICA

SOUTH AMERICA

ARG..................................ARGENTINA

EUROPE

AUT..................................AUSTRIA
BEL..................................BELGIUM
EST..................................ESTONIA
FIN..................................FINLAND
FRA..................................FRANCE
GBR..................................GREAT BRITAIN
GER..................................GERMANY
HUN..................................HUNGARY
ITA..................................ITALY
LIT..................................LITHUANIA
LUX..................................LUXEMBOURG
NED..................................THE NETHERLANDS
NOR..................................NORWAY
POL..................................POLAND
ROM..................................ROMANIA
SUI..................................SWITZERLAND
SWE..................................SWEDEN
TCH..................................CZECH REPUBLIC
YUG..................................YUGOSLAVIA

ASIA

JPN..................................JAPAN